T0091918

2D Graphics Programming
for Games

2D Graphics Programming
for Games

John Pile Jr

CRC Press
Taylor & Francis Group
Boca Raton London New York

CRC Press is an imprint of the
Taylor & Francis Group, an **informa** business

AN A K PETERS BOOK

CRC Press
Taylor & Francis Group
6000 Broken Sound Parkway NW, Suite 300
Boca Raton, FL 33487-2742

© 2013 by Taylor & Francis Group, LLC
CRC Press is an imprint of Taylor & Francis Group, an Informa business

No claim to original U.S. Government works

Printed on acid-free paper
Version Date: 20121220

International Standard Book Number: 978-1-4665-0189-8 (Hardback)

Library of Congress Cataloging-in-Publication Data

Pile, John, Jr.
  2D graphics programming for games / John Pile Jr.
    pages cm
  "An A K Peters book."
  Includes bibliographical references and index.
  ISBN 978-1-4665-0189-8 (alk. paper)
    1. Computer games--Programming. 2. Computer graphics. I. Title. II. Title: Two dimensional graphics programming for games.

  QA76.76.C672P49 2013
  794.8'1526--dc23   2012047939

Visit the Taylor & Francis Web site at
http://www.taylorandfrancis.com

and the CRC Press Web site at
http://www.crcpress.com

For Helen.

Contents

Preface

There are already some great books on programming 2D games, so why write one that focuses only on 2D graphics?

The answer is that whereas other books might succeed at covering a breadth of topics, they don't necessarily go into the depth required to make professional-looking games. Some great texts cover other advanced game development topics, such as game physics, game AI, real-time 3D graphics, and game architectures, but the information on 2D graphics has been difficult to find in a single text. Until now, that is.

Further, the books that do discuss the creation of 2D games focus on only one platform (OpenGL, DirectX, Flash, XNA). In reality, as you will see in this book, the core concepts of graphics programming are the same, regardless of platform.

Throughout this book you will learn the concepts and techniques used in making great 2D graphics. Much of what is included in this book might be considered general knowledge by many game developers, but those same developers would be at a loss to tell you where they actually picked up the information. The truth is that it has been gained by years of experience developing games.

When I was hired to teach a course on 2D graphics, I spent a great deal of time looking for a textbook that covered the topics I believe are most important for new game developers to learn. I could not find one, and the result is the content within this book.

My goal is that by the time you finish reading and working through the exercises in this text, you will be able to look at a game such as *Castle Crashers* [Zynga Dallas 11] and think, "Sure, I could do that."

In addition, I suspect you'll have a newfound respect for the roles of game artists and designers.

Acknowledgments

Among teaching, coding, and fulfilling a variety of other obligations, I have managed to finish writing a book during what is also my first two years of marriage. I therefore want to thank my beautiful wife, Helen, who has happily dealt with the glow of my computer screens until the wee hours of the morning and a year of too much work and not enough play.

I would also like thank my parents for their continual support and patience over the years. Even I am aware that having a middle-aged son who still plays computer games and watches cartoons is a little odd. Through the years, they have led by example, instilling a combined work and play ethic epitomized by my dad's motto: "Do what you love and the rest will follow." That has been my guiding principle and helps to explain why I look forward to each day of work.

At the end of this book are two appendices reviewing the basic math principles needed for this text, which are provided courtesy of Dr. Scott Stevens, Mathematics Coordinator at Champlain College. My thanks go out to him for putting these together. For further exploration of these topics, Scott developed an advanced course of the math needed for 3D game development. The textbook for that course, *Matrices, Vectors, and 3D Math*, is available online [Stevens 12].

My students also deserve a great deal of thanks. They keep me inspired and on my toes. Throughout this book you will find that many of the visual examples are screenshots of games created by my students. In addition, one of the great rewards of teaching at a time when all the latest software development information can be found online is that for those who want to learn, the classroom has now become an amazing two-way information exchange. When I give students a bit of background and point them in the right direction, they come back with all kinds of new and interesting stuff that I never could have found on my own.

Without sounding too much like an award speech, I want to give credit to the team I worked with at Proper Games: Mike, Danny, Andy, Fritz, Janek, Chris Bradwell, Chris Brown, Paddy, John, and, of course, Smithy. Additionally, much of the artwork in this book was provided by my Proper Games colleague and good friend Geoff Gunning. His unique artistic style and attention to detail are an inspiration. Geoff is truly a hidden talent and all-around good guy. I'm lucky to have had the privilege to work with him on almost every one of my major game projects.

Finally, I would like to thank two good friends who are gone too soon. Mike and Jenny, you are missed.

About the Author

John Pile Jr is a game developer and educator. He has taught courses in graphics, game physics, and game networking for the Game Studio at Champlain College since 2010. He holds a BS in mathematics from Fairmont State University and an MS in software engineering for computer game technology from the University of Abertay in Dundee, Scotland.

John also has an extensive career as a software engineer both in and out of the game industry, with credited titles for Xbox 360, PlayStation 3, PC, iOS, and Android. His most recently released title was *aliEnd* for Android.

While not teaching, writing books, or developing games, John spends his summers with his wife exploring his home state of Alaska, her home country of Scotland, and wherever else the wind might take them.

Part I

Getting Started in 2D

Chapter 1

Introduction

1.1 About This Book

This book is about programming, but at times also presents aspects of 2D graphics that might otherwise be considered more appropriate for a discussion on art or design. These are useful topics because they allow you, as a graphics programmer, to communicate effectively with both your art and design counterparts. They also give you the perspective to offer meaningful dialogue and suggestions on how a particular art or design challenge can be solved with a programmatic solution.

My emphasis in this book, as it is in my classroom, is threefold: theory, minimal code, and experimentation. By starting with a basic concept that demonstrates both the understanding of what we are trying to accomplish as well as why we are taking a particular approach, we set the proper context for the code we write. Minimal code samples allow the reader to see a particular line of code in action or as it relates to the code around it. These code samples are provided without the standard robustness of good coding standards. However, rest assure that this is done for the purpose of keeping the code consistent to a minimalist goal. A variety of texts are available on good coding practices for any language of choice, as well as on object-oriented programming and design patterns. Apply those principles to the code you write.

The final and most important part of my emphasis is experimentation. It has been my experience that most learning occurs when working through a problem, experimenting with solutions, and generally tinkering with code. The challenges listed in the book are for you to try. In addition to these challenges, other suggestions throughout the text present possible projects and added functionality. Take these suggestions to heart. The reader who experiments is the reader who learns.

1.1.1   Required Knowledge

This book assumes you already have a basic understanding of programming. The code samples listed in the text are written in C# but can easily be applied to most programming languages. When I teach this course at the college level, the students have only one year of C++ programming as their background. Assuming you already know Java, C++, or Objective-C, you should find the transition to C# fairly effortless.

The companion website, http://www.2dGraphicsProgramming.com, offers code samples in other programming languages. However, the focus of this book is on coding graphics, not the specifics of the language. To use a fairly bad analogy: when driving from Seattle to Florida, you need to understand the basic rules of the road and how to navigate, no matter what your vehicle. As long as you know how to drive at least one vehicle, the differences between driving a tractor or a sports car are irrelevant. Both vehicles need fuel and have an accelerator, brake, and transmission. As long as you can drive one, you will have the other figured out by the time you get there.

The text also assumes that the reader has a basic background in mathematics, including geometry and trigonometry. If it has been a while since your basic math days, the math primers in the appendices should help.

Be forewarned: the sample code included in the beginning of the text includes every line of code, but later you will be required to fill in the blanks yourself. Code snippets for a new concept are included, but after a while it is not necessary to repeat the same pieces of code for each sample.

1.1.2   Why 2D Games?

The last five years or so have demonstrated that it is still possible to create fun, addictive, and immersive game experiences in two dimensions. Runaway hits such as *Angry Birds* [Rovio Entertainment 09], *Peggle* [PopCap Games 07], and *Fruit Ninja* [Halfbrick Studios 10] are all examples of highly successful 2D games, and you probably can think of many more.

On a scale of realistic to symbolic, 2D games tend to fall to the symbolic side, although this is not always the case. These games speak to us on a more abstract level, and we are actually quite comfortable with that: we often communicate in 2D in the form of letters, numbers, symbols, and charts [Rasmussen 05].

In addition, some developers simply consider 2D a better platform for achieving certain artistic goals. Game artist Geoff Gunning put it this way: "I've never been a fan of 3D game art ... I can appreciate how impressive the talent is, but it never looks as characterful as 2D art."

Another important point is that 2D games usually require significantly less in art assets than their 3D counterparts. This can be a big deal for a small development team for whom resources are limited. But even in a 3D game, it is likely that some work is done in 2D. The user interface, heads-up display, and/or menuing system are likely rendered in 2D. In fact, unless a game is developed for a 3D television, games are still 2D media. The final output for most games is still a 2D screen.

Finally, from the perspective of someone who also loves to teach 3D graphics programming, I believe that focusing on 2D graphics is a great introduction to the broader graphics topics. In later chapters you will be able to create particle systems and write your own graphics shaders without the added confusion of 3D matrix math, lighting algorithms, and importing 3D models. I believe it is a valuable step in the learning process of those who want to become 3D graphics programmers to first understand 2D graphics thoroughly.

Beyond these justifications, 2D graphics are simply fun. They provide instant gratification and allow developers to quickly prototype ideas and mechanics.

1.2 Why C# and XNA?

The code samples included in this book are in C# with XNA. Every language has its advantages and disadvantages, but for the goals of this book, I strongly believe C#/XNA is the best choice for a number of reasons.

First, like Java, C# is a managed coding language. This means you won't get distracted by pointers and memory management. But, this comes at a cost. C# is not as fast as C++, however most platforms (even mobile devices) are able to handle this added overhead without that being much of an issue.

Second, using C#/XNA will allow your game to run natively on PCs (Windows), game consoles (Xbox 360), and even some mobile devices (Windows 7 Phone) without any significant modification. Then, with the help of an environment such as Mono, your C# game can easily be ported to Android, iOS, Mac PCs, Linux, and Sony platforms.

Let's pause for a moment here for emphasis because this second point should not be passed lightly. C#/XNA allows you to develop richly graphical games for almost any platform. Very few game development environments are able to make this same claim—and those that do come with their own set of challenges.

Third, XNA was created specifically for game development. It provides common structures and functions useful to game creation that are outside the scope of this text. At the same time, the tools provided by XNA are not so abstract that they become irrelevant to other platforms. For example, Unity3D has a great particle system, but using that particle system won't necessarily give you the experience to create your own.

Finally, XNA allows us to have direct access to the graphics card through the implementation of shader programming. This tool is powerful for creating advanced graphics effects, and the knowledge is easily transferable to both DirectX and OpenGL.

At the risk of repeating myself, the concepts discussed in this book are not specific to any one programming language or graphics library. This book is about understanding and exploring 2D graphics programming concepts; the language is just a means to an end.

1.2.1   Why not C++?

Before we get too far, I would like to address an often-cited reason for avoiding XNA. This is an idea that I see printed over and over, that *real game programming* is done in C++. Unfortunately, I have to admit that even a few years ago, I too was guilty of uttering that tired refrain.

The truth is that even though AAA game development almost always requires the programming performance available only through C++, we are quickly finding that a thriving new game market is being driven by non-AAA games. Combined with the power of modern multicore processors, most of these non-AAA games are being developed on a variety of non-C++ platforms.

That's not to say that you should avoid C++. It really is a powerful programming language that should be the foundation of any programming or computer science degree. However, we just don't need it for this text, and it could potentially provide an unnecessary barrier to many of the graphical concepts we cover here.

I have no doubt that we will continue to hear the "real game development" cliche in the future, but it comes from the same naysayers who claimed there was no future in online, social, mobile, or *indie* (independent video) games. It's just so 2006.

1.2.2   The Future of XNA

Another, more fundamental, concern with C# and XNA is that Microsoft appears to be on a path to sunset the XNA framework. Early in the discussion of Windows 8, there were rumors that the new operating system would not support XNA. Now that the operating system (OS) has been released, it is clear that there has been a specific choice not to provide direct support for XNA. Although games can be written to run on Windows 8–

based PCs, they cannot directly be deployed to Windows 8–based mobile devices and tablets.

While there is currently no team at Microsoft developing further versions of the XNA framework, their policy is to continue supporting software for ten years beyond the last point release. XNA 4.0 was released at the end of 2011 and I have been assured by my friends at Microsoft that XNA will be supported until at least 2021. Just know that we may need to do a little extra work to prepare our XNA game for Windows 8 devices and associate marketplace.

The good news is that there is a path to publishing XNA games on Windows 8 mobile devices via Mono and MonoGame (the same technology that allows us to use the XNA framework on Android devices, which conveniently also happen to run the ARM architecture).

The future of XNA might remain uncertain, but for now I am quite content that, as a game developer, the framework meets my cross-platform 2D game development needs. And if something better does comes along, I'll be the first to give it a try.

1.2.3 Required Software

Microsoft provides the developer tools for free. To run the code samples in this book, you will need (at a minimum)

- Visual C# Express 2010,

- XNA Game Studio 4.0.

These development tools are available for download. It may be easiest to get them directly from http://create.msdn.com; I have also provided a link on the book's companion website http://www.2dGraphicsProgramming.com in case that ever changes.

In addition to the required software, I suggest you become familiar with graphics tools, including Adobe Photoshop or the open source alternative Gimp. Knowing how to work with these tools, even if only to do minor edits such as resizing, will help you in the long run. It is well worth knowing the tools of the artist.

1.2.4 An Artistic Programmer

The common perception is that there is a dichotomy between the creative artist and the logical programmer—right-brained versus left-brained, cold and calculating versus warm, fuzzy, and touchy-feely. And even though I might argue that these stereotypes are unfair in any setting, the best attributes of both are required in game development when programming graphics for games.

The rest of this chapter provides some background for those who are truly new to game development. For the rest of you, feel free to jump to Chapter 2, where we take our first "byte" into computer graphics.

1.3   Game Development 101

Making games is fun, but its also difficult. My point is that making games requires specialized skills, and with rare exceptions,[1] even the most simple game project needs at least an artist and a programmer. At its core, that's what this book is about: the relationship between the artist and the programmer—as well as the skills, tools, and tricks that will help make the best game possible.

In most cases, a more typical development team will include a variety of other talented people. From designer to publisher, quality assurance to marketing, there are a range of skilled professionals that large-scale development budgets can afford. It is worth taking a brief look at the varying skills required for game development.

- **Programmer:** A programmer is someone who writes computer software. Simply put, it's the programmer's responsibility to ensure the game works. In the early days of game development, game programmers did all the work (art, design, and coding). Today, those typical roles are spread across the development team, and there are specializations within the field of programming. These may include game engine programming, graphics programming, artificial intelligence, and game-play programming; even audio programming has become its own specialization. On a smaller development team, a programmer may be expected to work on just about any part of the game. If one thing is certain: when the game breaks, it is the programmer who is called in to fix it.

- **Artist:** Game artists fall into a variety of categories and specializations, but art is the key. The skills among artists are quite divergent, especially when comparing 2D and 3D game artists—the skills of the 2D artist may be completely foreign to those of an accomplished 3D modeler or animator (and vice versa). However, whatever the specialization, a good game artist will have aesthetic sensibilities and a sense of color and style. Technical skills in an artist are highly valued but not always required.

---

[1]Game engines such as Unity3D have allowed single individuals to create polished games for the iOS (e.g., *Colorbind* [Lutz 10]).

- **Designer:** The game designer has the responsibility of making the game into a *game*. The designer is the first to be praised on the successes and the first to be blamed when the game does not live up to expectations. Whereas the programmers build the systems and the artists create the style, the game designer is tasked with the responsibility of ensuring the entire experience is compelling, balanced, interesting, and/or rewarding. From the initial concepts to fine tuning the game mechanics to the tedious details of ensuring each game level is challenging without being too difficult, the game designer must be a jack-of-all-trades.

- **Additional roles:** A variety of other roles and tasks have the potential to become full-time positions, depending on the size of the team and the project. These roles typically include a *producer* to manage the project and deal with outside forces as well as a *quality assurance lead* to ensure the game is thoroughly tested before it is shipped. Games may also require audio technicians, voice actors, information support system engineers, website developers, server administrators—the list goes on.

1.4   Game Developer Platforms

The topics covered in this text can easily be applied to many game platforms. This section highlights the differences in programming on various platforms. This is not meant to be a complete survey of the field (the list is always growing), but it should serve to describe some of the various options for 2D game development. Again, the topics covered in this text can easily be applied to any of the following.

1.4.1   Adobe Flash

Flash is a great platform for developing games; however, with the advent of mobile devices, Adobe has had to modify its strategy. Even though Flash games are not a great choice for web-based mobile development due to lack of support as well as in-browser performance issues, you can create games in Flash and deploy them as native applications on mobile devices. Flash is a great platform for building 2D user interfaces through products like Autodesk's Scaleform. In addition, Flash is a very powerful art tool and can be the primary tool for 2D artists when building game animations.

1.4.2   HTML 5 and JavaScript

HTML 5 has emerged as a possible platform to fill the need for browser-based games. Although performance issues still remain, a large number of developers are having significant success developing sprite-based games with HTML 5. The biggest advantage for HTML 5 and JavaScript development is the potential for huge cross-platform access through a web browser. The idea is that anything that has a web browser (which is just about everything) is now capable of running your game. Unfortunately, there are still minor issues with HTML 5 support on older Android devices. Microsoft is pushing HTML 5 as a potential development environment for native Windows 8 apps, and the ubiquitous nature of freemium games means that the old arguments about the difficulties of monetizing browser-based games are no longer valid arguments for avoiding the platform.

1.4.3   iOS

To date, iOS 5.0 is the latest operating system available for the various iDevices such as iPads, iPods, and iPhones. A variety of great resources exist for learning how to develop on iOS; the details are beyond the scope of this book. However, these devices are all OpenGL compliant. As previously mentioned, MonoGame is a great tool for porting the XNA framework onto an iOS device. In addition, a variety of game engines will generate native code that can deploy to iOS devices, including Unity3D, cocos2d, Corona SDK, and even Flash.

1.4.4   Android

Even though there are reportedly more Android devices (including Kindles, Nooks, the Ouya game console, and thousands of tablets and phones) than iOS mobile devices, the Apple Marketplace remains the best and most profitable market for most mobile game developers. The Android market remains the "Wild West" for developers attempting to fight piracy while trying to maintain support for a never-ending list of device sizes, OS versions, and marketplaces. Like browser-based game development, the *freemium model* remains one of the few ways to make a profit. Game development for Android is helped through the same engines as for iOS devices, including Unity3D, cocos2d, Corona SDK, and Flash. If you want to start from scratch, however, you can write your game in Java and OpenGL. My advice is still to develop games for Android via XNA through MonoGame.

1.4.5 Xbox 360

Presently, XNA remains the only way for non-Microsoft partners to develop for the Xbox 360. The XNA framework was originally launched as just that—a way to write games for the console—and the Xbox Marketplace remains an active location to build, test, and publish indie games. Support for the Xbox 360 is a native feature of the XNA framework, and once your account is activated, you can have a simple game demo running on the console in just a few minutes.

1.4.6 Graphics Libraries

The two primary graphics libraries for interacting with graphics hardware are OpenGL and DirectX. Commercial graphics cards are almost always both OpenGL and DirectX compatible, although mobile devices are changing the landscape. Historically, both OpenGL and DirectX APIs were predominately accessed through C++ interfaces. That has now changed, however, and OpenGL is accessed through Objective-C on iOS devices and through Java on Android devices. Recently, mobile devices have begun to support programmable GPUs, but in many cases shader programming is still limited to PC and console game development.

OpenGL. OpenGL is an open source graphics library that is maintained by the Khronos Group. Until recently, OpenGL was primarily seen as a great tool for scientists and 3D simulators, but not necessarily the best choice for game developers. This opinion existed for two reasons. First, unlike DirectX, the OpenGL library is specific to only graphics. You need a separate library to access input controllers, audio, and other game-specific features. Second, since Microsoft Windows was the dominant operating system on the market, there was not a significant demand for developing games in anything other than Microsoft's proprietary graphics library. However, this all changed with the release and commercial success of the iPhone as a gaming device. OpenGL ES, the light version of the full desktop implementation of OpenGL, is now the graphics library of choice for mobile development, including both iOS and Android devices. Additionally, OpenGL graphics libraries will run across all platforms, including Microsoft Windows and Linux distributions. OpenGL provides support for programmable GPUs through its shader language GLSL (Graphics Library Shader Language).

DirectX. DirectX has been Microsoft's "catch all" for all game-related APIs and libraries, including DirectDraw (the 2D graphics API) and Direct3D. Unlike OpenGL, DirectX has always been primarily focused on game development and includes a variety of rich features for games, including support for 3D audio and game controllers. Although newer versions of DirectX have been released and are regularly pushed by vendors at conferences, until recently DirectX 9.0c was a staple of the game industry because it was the most recent version of DirectX that would run on all Xbox 360 hardware. DirectX provides support for programmable GPUs through its shader language HLSL (High-Level Shading Language).

XNA Framework. XNA is built on the foundation of DirectX. Although initially limited, recent releases of the XNA framework have become much more closely aligned with its DirectX foundation. XNA is more than a set of APIs, however; it is a full framework designed specifically for making games and built on the strengths of the C# language. It provides an asset pipeline for importing and working with a variety of game assets, including audio (both music and sound effects), portable network graphics (PNG) images, and XML data files. The developers of the framework have created a system that does the heavy lifting of common game tasks and provides a great base for building game systems. Often mistaken by nonprogrammers as a game engine, XNA does not provide the high-level user interface that might be found in Unity3D or the Unreal Development Kit (UDK). Instead, XNA still requires strong programming and software engineering skills. This additional requirement means that it also remains extremely flexible, and developers have access to the entire C# and .NET libraries if desired. Like DirectX, the XNA framework provides support for programmable GPUs through HLSL.

1.5   Book Organization

1.5.1   Sample Code

As a teacher, I believe students often rely on sample code as a crutch. The goal of code samples should be to give enough to get started but not to give away the fun of solving the problem. As a result, the sample code provided in this book is focused on the task at hand.

   As you work your way through the book, I suggest you implement good coding practices as you build your graphics system. The code samples demonstrate the subject in a way to make it understandable. This often may not be the best or most efficient solution, so suggestions for building more robust graphics systems and improving efficiency in your code are included.

   The code samples provided in the book are shown in C# and XNA, but in most cases they require only minor modifications to implement them in other languages. The website http://www.2dGraphicsProgramming.com provides code samples in raw OpenGL, DirectX, and Flash.

1.5.2 Exercises: Questions

The exercise questions serve to test your understanding of the major topics discussed in the chapter. If you are able to answer these questions successfully, you will know you are well on your way to learning the essentials.

1.5.3 Exercises: Challenges

If you're like me, you may just want to get to coding. The "Challenges" present programming challenges that allow you to apply what you have learned in the chapter. They are designed to get you thinking about the application of the topics and often result in tools or sample code that can be used in later projects.

Chapter 2

Basics of Computer Graphics

This chapter presents a brief overview of how simple images are stored and displayed on the screen, especially as computer graphics impacts modern game development. It is by no means a complete story. During the early days of computer graphics, a variety of rather complicated hardware and software tricks were employed by game console manufacturers to display moving images on a television screen. Techniques such as "racing the beam" allowed programmers to extend the capabilities of very limited hardware. Although interesting, the details are not relevant to modern game development and are beyond the scope of this text. Instead, this chapter focuses on some basic theories and implementations of the standard graphics techniques used today.

2.1 Bits and Bytes

Starting at the most basic level, computers use 1s and 0s to store information. The value (1 or 0) is stored in a *bit*, analogous to a light bulb that is either on or off. Series of bits are used to store larger numbers, in which each number column represents a power of 2. This binary number system is the basis for modern computing, but, as you can imagine, it is not very convenient for humans. As seen below, we need four digits just to display the number 15:

$$0000 = 0, \quad 0001 = 1, \quad 0010 = 2, \quad 0011 = 3, \quad \ldots, \quad 1111 = 15.$$

To make things a bit easier, we group our binary numbers into blocks of 4 bits. Each group of 4 bits has 16 unique combinations of 0s and 1s (0000 to 1111), corresponding to the decimal numbers 0 to 15. As a matter of convenience, we can write these 16 combinations into a single "digit" by using the hexadecimal number system (base 16), in which decimal 10 is hexadecimal A, 11 is B, and so on. In hexadecimal, then, we can count to 15 as

0, 1, 2, 3, 4, 5, 6, 7, 8, 9, A, B, C, D, E, F.

A group of 8 bits (called a *byte*) can store 256 unique combinations of bits (0000 0000 to 1111 1111) and can also be more easily written by using the hexadecimal number system of 00 to FF. In counting upward, when reaching F in the rightmost digit, we start over with 0 in the right digit and add 1 to the left digit until we reach FF (just as 39 is followed by 40 when counting upward in the decimal system):

00, 01, 02, ... 09, 0A, 0B, 0C, 0D, 0E, 0F, 10, 11, ... FD, FE, FF.

If you're feeling a bit overwhelmed by all these numbers (pun intended), don't worry. You'll soon see the reason for this review of introductory computer science.

2.1.1 Digital Color Theory

```
000000
010010
000000
100001
011110
000000
```

Figure 2.1. Thirty-six bits aligned in rows.

The simplest (and perhaps most obvious) way to store a graphical image is as a two-dimensional array of colors. Or, as in the following example, an array of bits.

Consider the following array of 36 bits:

000000 010010 000000 100001 011110 000000.

By aligning the array of 36 bits into 6 rows of 6 bits, as shown in Figure 2.1, we can build the image shown in Figure 2.2 where a 0 bit represents white and a 1 bit represents black.

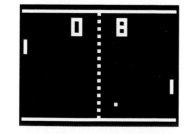

Figure 2.2. Bitmap from 36 bits.

This type of black and white "1 bits per pixel (bpp) color" was used in early games such as Atari's *Pong* (Figure 2.3) and later in the *graphical user interface* (GUI) for the Apple Macintosh OS (Figure 2.4). This two-dimensional map of bits is where we get the term *bitmap*.

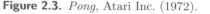

Figure 2.3. *Pong*, Atari Inc. (1972).   **Figure 2.4.** Mac 128k, Apple Inc. (1984).

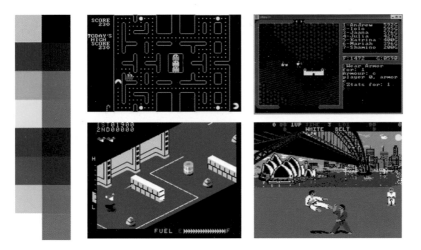

Figure 2.5. The 4-bit color palette (right) and some 4-bit games (clockwise from top left): Namco's *Pac-Man* (1980), Origin Systems' *Ultima IV* (1985), *Bruce Lee* (1984), and Sega's *Zaxxon* (1982).

The decade between *Pong* and the Macintosh did see significant advances in game graphics. By 1977, the Atari 2600 game system featured a palette of 128 available colors. Advances in this era were achieved through a variety of creative hardware and software techniques, allowing programmers to stretch the limits of game consoles. At the time, RAM was too significantly expensive to allow for a single bit in memory to represent every pixel on the screen. Instead, games had to reuse the same collection of bits (called a *sprite*) so that the same chunk of memory could be used multiple times (sometimes flipping or stretching it) to fill the game screen. It wasn't until the early 1980s that we began to see personal computers with dedicated video RAM for displaying a 2D array of colors directly to the screen. However, the use of sprites was convenient and continues through today. We'll take a closer look at sprites in Chapter 3.

IBM's Color Graphics Adapter (CGA) featured 16 kilobytes of memory, capable of displaying either a 2-bit *color depth* (4 colors) at 320 pixels wide by 200 pixels high or a 4-bit color depth (16 colors) at 160×200:

$$2\, \frac{\text{bits}}{\text{pixel}} \times (320 \times 200)\ \text{pixels} = 128{,}000\ \text{bits} = 16{,}000\ \text{bytes},$$

$$4\, \frac{\text{bits}}{\text{pixel}} \times (160 \times 200)\ \text{pixels} = 128{,}000\ \text{bits} = 16{,}000\ \text{bytes}.$$

These early graphical systems implemented a specific set of colors that could be use in developing software for their system. Figure 2.5 shows an example of a 4-bit color palette. Depending on the system, this usually included 8 colors (black, red, green, yellow, blue, magenta, cyan, and white) in both low and high intensity, providing for 16 colors. In some cases, the developer could set a specific color palette to use for a particular game, allowing for at least some color variety between titles.

As hardware became cheaper, software developers soon had access to greater color depth. Doubling the depth from 4 bpp to 8 bpp allowed a move from 16 colors to a full palette of 256 colors. Now there was the new challenge of dealing with all those colors in a way that made sense.

2.1.2   RGB Color Model

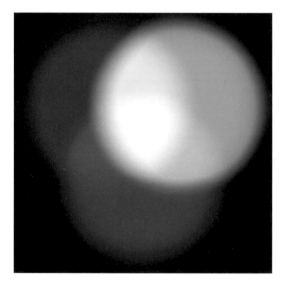

Figure 2.6. RGB colors combined: magenta, yellow, cyan, and white are all clearly visible in the intersections of red, green, and blue.

Let's take a quick side step and look at the way computer monitors works. First, let's look at the traditional CRT computer monitor (the heavy ones with the large cone-shaped back, which were typical in the 1980s and 1990s). As with CRT televisions, CRT computer monitors send a stream of electrons that bombard a net of phosphors located on the back of the computer screen. A *phosphor* is simply a substance that illuminates light when hit with an electron. Tiny red, green, and blue (*RGB*) phosphors group together to form what we would consider a single pixel. (See Figures 2.6 and 2.7.)

In the more modern LCD screens, the same concept is used, but instead of a ray of electrons and phosphors, LCD monitors make use of the light-emitting properties of liquid crystals. Again, the chosen colors are red, green, and blue.

In both CRT and LED screens, the colors red, green, and blue are combined in a small point to create the color of each pixel on the screen. These combinations blend together to form all the colors we need.

If you have a background in traditional painting, you may know that from an artist's perspective, red, yellow, and blue are the primary colors. Then why not use red, yellow, and blue light instead of RGB?

Actually, the human eye also works by combining RGB light. As you can see in Figure 2.8, the human eye comprises millions of red, green, and blue light-sensitive cones. The red cones allow us to perceive red light; the green cones, green light; and the blue cones, blue light. Combined, these cones allow us to see all the colors of the rainbow.

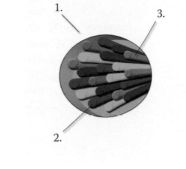

Figure 2.7. The surface of a CRT monitor is covered with red, green, and blue phosphors that glow when energized.

Figure 2.8. Cross section of light-sensitive rods and cones that permeate the surface of the human retina: (1) retina, (2) cones, and (3) rods.

In addition to the color-sensitive cones, the retina of the eye also has rods, which work best in low light conditions. This is why colors will seem more vivid in the light of day.

Therefore, it made sense to use the same RGB color model to store color data in the computer's memory. So in the move to 12-bit color depth, instead of simply defining an arbitrary palette of 4,096 colors, game developers could now divide those 12 bits into groups so that 4 bits were available to each of the three colors in a color computer monitor:

$$12 \ \frac{\text{bits}}{\text{pixel}} = 4 \text{ bits red} + 4 \text{ bits green} + 4 \text{ bits blue}.$$

From three 0s (R = G = B = 0) to three 15s (R = G = B = 15), we suddenly had an easy convention for managing 4,096 combinations of the RGB colors. Conveniently, these values can be recorded hexadecimally: for example,

- F00 (red),
- 0F0 (green),
- 00F (blue),
- 000 (black),
- 888 (gray),
- FFF (white),
- AAF (dark blue),
- 44F (light blue),
- 808 (purple).

Even though 12-bit color is good, it doesn't provide enough colors to create photographic-quality images. As a result, once the hardware became affordable, 12-bit RBG color was followed by color depths of 16-bit (commonly referred to as *high color*) and eventually 24-bit (*true color*). See Figure 2.9. The 24-bit color allows a full 8 bits (1 byte) per RGB color channel, resulting in more than 16 million color combinations.

Some RGB formats	
12-bit RGB (4096 colors)	$16 \times 16 \times 16$
---- ---- ----	
16-bit RGB (65,536 colors)	$32 \times 64 \times 32$
- ---- -- ---- - ----	(High Color)
24-bit RGB (16.7 million)	$256 \times 256 \times 256$
---- ---- ---- ---- ---- ----	(True Color)

Figure 2.9. RGB colors combined.

In other fields it may be necessary to go beyond 24-bit RGB color (the bitmap filetype supports up to 64 bpp), but the current standard for game development is 8 bits per color channel:

$$24 \ \frac{\text{bits}}{\text{pixel}} = 8 \text{ bits red} + 8 \text{ bits green} + 8 \text{ bits blue}.$$

Figure 2.10 shows an example of a photograph rendered at various color depths.

Defining colors in terms of various amounts of red, green, and blue is convenient and has become a game industry standard, but it is not the only way to define a color. In fact, the human eye does not see those three colors evenly. When viewing Figure 2.11, you may notice that your eye can see more detail in the green gradient when compared to the red or blue gradients. For that reason, when 16-bit RGB color was introduced and the bits could not be easily divided among the three components, it made sense to give the remaining bit to green.

Figure 2.10. The same photograph at 1 bpp (left), 8 bpp (center), and 24 bpp (right).

Figure 2.11. RGB gradients: you will likely detect more detail in the green band than in the red or blue bands.

2.1.3 RGBA: Blending with Alpha

With 256 options per channel, the permutations of the 24-bit RGB color model provide for a significant variety of colors (16.7 million colors per pixel):

$$16,777,216 \text{ colors} =$$
$$256 \text{ shades of red} \times 256 \text{ shades of green} \times 256 \text{ shades of blue}.$$

In the real world, however, not all materials are completely opaque; some surfaces allow light through (picture a pair of red-tinted glasses sitting on a blue tablecloth). In computer graphics, we can store how "transparent" a pixel is in a fourth byte called the *alpha value*. Since artists want to layer images within a game, the color model would not be complete without transparency.

An 8-bit alpha value is convenient because it allows an additional 256 shades of transparency to the base RGB color scheme, forming the *RGBA* color scheme. An alpha value of 255 represents a pixel that is fully opaque, and a value of 0 signifies a pixel that is completely transparent. The exact algorithm for determining how overlapping transparent pixels are blended together is discussed in Chapter 8.

With the 32-bit RGBA color palette, we now have the ability to store more than 4 billion color combinations in just 4 bytes of memory. That's more than enough for most applications, and a far distance from the two colors from the beginning of this chapter. But now we have another potential problem: the memory required for an 800×600 image, which is

$$1.92 \text{ MB} = 800 \text{ pixels} \times 600 \text{ pixels} \times 4 \, \frac{\text{bytes}}{\text{pixel}}.$$

Notice the switch from bits per pixel (bpp) to *bytes per pixel* (Bpp).

2.1.4   First XNA Project

Building your first XNA project is very simple by using the built-in templates and the XNA framework game class. Once you have installed Visual C# Express 2010 and Microsoft XNA Game Studio 4.0, simply start Visual C# Express. Select File → New Project from the toolbar.

In the dialog box, choose Installed Templates → Visual C# → XNA Game Studio 4.0 → Windows Game (4.0). Check that you're happy with the project name and file location, and then click OK.

Within the game class created by the template, you will notice a constructor and five overridden functions for initialization, content load, content unload, update, and draw. The XNA framework is defined so that the update and draw functions are called at an appropriate *frame rate* (frames per second, or fps) for the given platform (60 fps for PC and Xbox, 30 fps for Windows Phone).

Press F5 to start debugging, and you should soon see a light blue game window.

2.1.5   XNA Corner

XNA has a built-in 32-bit color structure for defining red, green, blue, and alpha byte values. In addition to the R, G, B, and A accessors, the structure includes a variety of predefined named colors. As of XNA Game Studio 4.0, this includes 142 colors from Alice blue (R: 240; G: 248; B: 255; A: 255) to yellow green (R: 154; G: 205; B: 50; A: 255).

To demonstrate, temporarily add the following code to your Initialize function:

```
1   //Color values example

    Color myColor = Color.DarkOliveGreen;

5   Console.WriteLine("Color values for DarkOliveGreen");
    Console.WriteLine(" Red:   " + myColor.R);
    Console.WriteLine(" Green: " + myColor.G);
    Console.WriteLine(" Blue:  " + myColor.B);
    Console.WriteLine(" Alpha: " + myColor.A);
```

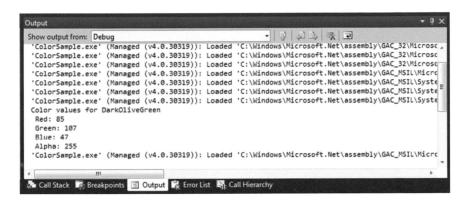

Figure 2.12. Output screenshot.

When running your project, you will notice the output in the console window similar to that shown in Figure 2.12. The choice of colors and associated RGBA values seems a bit arbitrary and not necessarily very useful for game development. Instead, we'll rely on our artist to use colors within sprites and then we'll use numeric values to programmatically modify the color RGBA accessors at runtime.

Microsoft XNA samples use the default color of cornflower blue (R: 100; G: 149; B: 237; A: 255), which has become synonymous with *programmer art*. A quick search for the text "CornflowerBlue" in the XNA template shows that it is used as the clear color in the Draw function.

2.1.6 Raster versus Vector Graphics

The term for the type of bitmap graphics we have discussed so far is *raster graphics*. The term derives its name from the way images were originally drawn on a television monitor, but it now has a more generalized meaning to describe graphics comprised of a rectangular grid of pixels.

Storing raster graphics can take up a lot of space in memory, but they have another disadvantage (consider Figure 2.13). When the sprite is enlarged, the image appears pixelated. A similar (although sometimes less noticeable) loss of detail occurs even when the image is made smaller. In some cases this may be acceptable, but in others you'll need your artist to make multiple copies of your images, rendered at the appropriate sizes.

An alternative is *vector graphics*, which uses mathematical formulas and the computational power of the computer to draw the exact shape you want at the exact resolution you need. For example, if you need to draw a line, you would need only the start and end points of the line and then to tell the computer to render pixels at all the points in between.

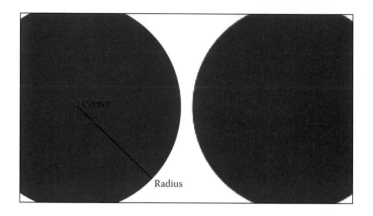

Figure 2.13. An enlarged vector circle (left); note the pixel-perfect smooth edge. An enlarged raster circle (right); note the jagged edge.

Alternatively, to render a solid circle, you simply need to track a center location and the radius. For every pixel in the scene, simply check the distance to the center of the circle. If it is less than or equal to the radius, then color the pixel with the appropriate color.

Vector graphics comes with both advantages and disadvantages, and the details of how to use it could fill a book. In this text, the closest we will get is with splines in Section 10.3.

2.2 Display

2.2.1 UV Coordinates

Often various-sized source images will be used for deploying the same game to various platforms. For example, large textures may be used when deploying the game to a desktop computer with a powerful graphics card, whereas smaller textures may be used when deploying the same game to mobile devices. In these cases, it can make sense to normalize (see Appendix B.4) the coordinate system so that the top-left pixel is set to be $(0, 0)$ and the bottom-right pixel is set to be $(1, 1)$. As a result, any individual *texel* can be measured in terms of percentage from the origin along the U (normalized X) and V (normalized Y) axes. (Texel is the term for a pixel on a texture.)

For example, an individual texel located at the coordinates $(512, 512)$ on a texture that measures $1{,}024 \times 1{,}024$ will have *UV-coordinates* of $(0.5, 0.5)$. Measuring texel locations in terms of UV coordinates instead of with *XY-coordinates* ensures that the location values are independent of the texture size.

UV coordinates are most often used in 3D graphics; it also helps to distinguish between the UV-axes on the source textures and the XYZ-axes within the 3D game world. This same normalization of the axes occurs when working with pixel shaders (see Section 9.3).

For the purposes of clarity, the examples in this book use nonnormalized XY-coordinates when working with textures.

2.2.2 Image Resolution

Thus far, we have explored the ability to increase the quality of an image by increasing the range of possible colors for each pixel. Another option is to simply increase the number of pixels. This may seem obvious, but let's consider Figures 2.14 and 2.15. Figure 2.14 is rendered at 400 pixels wide, and Figure 2.15 is 200 pixels wide. By doubling the pixel width (assuming we're constraining the image proportions), we need four times the amount of storage space:

$$\text{New storage} = (2 \times \text{width}) \times (2 \times \text{height}) \times \frac{\text{bytes}}{\text{pixel}}.$$

Figure 2.14. 400×278.

Note that some artists (especially those with a graphic design or print background) think of images as a combination of *pixel density* and final physical width on the screen (rather than as simple pixel resolution). Since Figures 2.14 and 2.15 are rendered to the same physical width on the page, Figure 2.14 has twice the pixel density of Figure 2.15. On modern game platforms, it is not common practice to scale images in a 2D game; game artists will expect a 1:1 relationship between the pixels in the images they create and how those pixels result on screen.

Figure 2.15. 200×139.

As a result, graphics programmers have historically discussed games only in terms of their pixel resolution. When developing games for a game console, developers know players will be playing their games on either *standard definition televisions* (SDTV) or *high definition televisions* (HDTV). Assuming an HDTV, developers ensure their games will render at 1,280 × 720 (a typical resolution for HDTVs).

In this scenario, the developers do not need to worry about the actual size of the screen. Whether the player's game console is connected to a 20-inch TV set or the game is displayed on a wall through an HD projector, the resolution is still 1,280 × 720. Similarly, a game on a PC is rendered at a specific resolution. If that resolution is smaller than the screen size, the game is rendered in a window. If the player chooses to switch the game to full-screen mode, the computer's hardware and operating system handle the appropriate upscaling of the game onto the PC monitor.

Occasionally, 2D games are required to support multiple graphical resolutions. For a console game, this is done so the game can support both SDTV and HDTV. Since modern game consoles have enough computing power to deal with the higher resolution, it has become common practice to generate game assets only at high resolution and then simply scale the final game image for the smaller screen. In some cases, such as porting a game to run on a very low-end PC, the art assets need to be scaled down to an appropriate size before the game is shipped. In these cases, the game is programmed to detect the game hardware and then select the appropriate art assets. (An exception must be made for font sizes, because we never want the text scaled so small that it becomes unreadable.)

With the move toward game development on tablet computers and other mobile devices, however, this is changing. The pixel density on these devices is increasing to the point where the human eye cannot detect individual pixels, so game developers now need to decide whether they really want their 720 pixels shoved onto a two-inch wide screen. Even though all the pixels are still there, is the image now too small? Although "too many pixels" may be a good problem to have, it's still something that graphics programmers need to understand and know how to handle. We'll look in more detail at scaling in Chapter 3.

2.2.3 Aspect Ratio

A measure of the relationship of width to height (W:H), *aspect ratio* is often discussed in terms of television displays. For decades, SDTVs displayed images at an aspect ratio of 4:3 (1.33:1), the width being one-third greater in length than the height. This aspect ratio was common also in computer monitors, resulting in resolutions that hold the same aspect ratio (400 × 300, 640 × 480, 800 × 600, and 1,024 × 768).

At the same time, feature films are often shot in the much wider aspect ratio of 1.85:1, and this has been the standard for US theaters since the 1960s. The advantage of the wider aspect ratio is the ability to display an image in a way that better matches the way we see the world.

With the advent of high-definition displays has come a move toward a wider aspect ratio. As mentioned earlier, the typical 1,280 × 720 HDTV resolution is now common, with an aspect ratio of 16:9 (1.78:1). We see the same move in computer monitors, with many wide-screen monitors running resolutions to match the HDTV aspect ratio (1,280 × 720, 1,600 × 900, and 1,920 × 1,080). Compare the various aspect ratios shown in Figure 2.16.

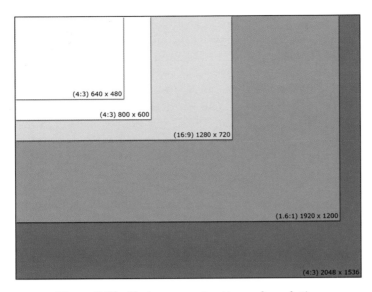

Figure 2.16. Various aspect ratios and resolutions

2.2.4 Mobile Displays

Since the recent introduction of the iPhone and the subsequent mobile game boom, we have seen an incredible "mobile arms race" between Apple, its competitors, and even itself.

Device	Resolution	Aspect	Release Date
Apple iPhone	480 × 320	1.5:1	29-06-2007
Apple iPad	1,024 × 768	1.3:1	03-04-2010
Google Nexus One	800 × 480	1.67:1	05-01-2010
Apple iPhone 4s	960 × 640	1.5:1	24-06-2010
Amazon Kindle Fire	1,024 × 600	1.7:1	15-11-2011
Apple iPad 3	2.048 × 1.536	1.3:1	13-03-2012
Samsung Galaxy S III	1.280 × 720	1.78:1	29-04-2012
Amazon Kindle Fire HD	1,280 × 800	1.6:1	14-09-2012
Apple iPhone 5	1,136 × 640	1.78:1	21-09-2012
Apple iPad Mini	1,024 × 768	1.3:1	02-11-2012

The resultant constantly morphing expectations for resolution and aspect ratios have made for a very difficult situation for game developers in the mobile market. Current devices have anywhere from 320,000 to 3.1 million pixels, with aspect ratios varying from 1.3:1 to 1.78:1.

In the case of the latest full-size iPads, the resolution of 2,048 × 1,536 is significantly larger than that of HDTVs. While providing some amazing potential for game display, this resolution is problematically even higher than the monitors used by most game developers. Not only is there the obvious problem of the huge resolution on art resources, there also is an expectation that the game will deploy and make use of both the low and high ends of the pixel spectrum. This may mean multiple size art assets that must be packaged with the mobile game.

These new issues associated with resolution versus physical width became apparent during the development of *aliEnd*. We had originally planned the game for the Xbox 360, but as the project neared completion, it was evident that mobile devices provided a really cool mechanic for the game. At the time, I was experimenting with the Windows phone development and decided that *aliEnd* provided a perfect opportunity to test out Microsoft's claim that an XNA game would easily port to the phone.

Even though the game functioned great on the mobile device, the artist, Geoff Gunning, wasn't happy with the way it looked on the small device. All the personality he had lovingly embodied frame by frame into the game characters was lost on the tiny screen. I later compared it to an actor moving from television to the Broadway stage—the subtle facial expressions are lost on those in the back rows. The solution of zooming in on the character was a fairly simple solution, but we lucked out. Had the original view been necessary for the game play, we would have faced a fairly difficult problem.

2.2.5 Console Standards

Before we leave the topic of resolution, it is worth noting one other difference in the old analog SDTV. That is, there are actually three primary standards in place: NTSC (developed in the United States and primarily used in the Americas and various other locations), SECAM (developed in Europe and adopted for use in various European and Asian countries), and PAL (developed in Germany—it eventually became the standard for all of Europe and Russia). Even though developers now make games targeted for HDTV systems, the Xbox 360, PlayStation 3, and Wii generation of game consoles still need to connect with those older standards. The result is that console games are often released based on their geographic region. Combined with DVD region coding, languages, and rating bodies that vary from country to country, publishing games for consoles can be a fairly significant undertaking. Whereas issues surrounding languages and ratings still exist for mobile development, development tasks due to analog television standards and DVD regions thankfully are not an issue for mobile and PC development.

2.2.6   Frame Rate

The *frame rate* is a measure of the number of screen draws (frames) per second. Console players will expect a minimum of 60 fps for action games, and the limited graphics hardware in mobile devices will often see acceptable frame rates of 30 fps. In old animation clips, 12 fps was considered the lowest acceptable frame rate, although today it would look fairly bad if the entire screen was updating at such a slow speed.

Keeping track of the current frame rate is important because it will allow you to quickly learn whether you have written any poor performing code. You can keep track by creating a counter that is incremented every time the Draw function is executed. Then, once a second has passed, update your frame rate with the number of frames counted over the last second.

```
1   double m_iElapsedMilliseconds = 0;
    int m_iFrameCount = 0;
    int m_iFPS = 0;

5   public void Update(GameTime gameTime)
    {
      m_iElapsedMilliseconds += gameTime.ElapsedGameTime.
        TotalMilliseconds;

      if (m_iElapsedMilliseconds > 1000)
10    {
        m_iElapsedMilliseconds -= 1000;
        m_iFPS = m_iFrameCount;
        m_iFrameCount = 0;
      }
15
      //Update Game
      //...
    }

20  public void Draw(GameTime gameTime)
    {
      m_iFrameCount++;
      Console.WriteLine("FPS is: " + m_iFPS);

25    //Draw Scene
      //...
    }
```

Running at 60 fps means that the frame should be drawn every 17 milliseconds (ms). The game update may run faster or slower than 60 fps, but it is important to try to hold the draw rate at 60 fps. If not, the player will notice.

As a result, if any significant operations occur during your game update that take longer than 17 ms (for example, texture or audio content loading, save game operations, artificial intelligence calculations, or leaderboard updates), it is important that these do not block the game draw from occurring.

One option is to divide the work across multiple frames. For example, if you know your path-finding algorithm may take up to 60 ms, you could pause the path-finding algorithm after 10 ms and then resume the path-finding calculations on the next frame. Depending on your system architecture, a better option may be to offload the intensive calculations to other nonblocking processor threads.

Ensuring background operations do not prevent the game Draw function from occurring is especially important when saving games or querying remote databases. In these circumstances, you should always use asynchronous function calls if they are available.

2.3   Double Buffering

Drawing images to the screen is fast, but our eyes are fast too. Imagine we were to draw a background image and then quickly draw another image on top of it to hide the background. The goal here is to create a final scene in which some piece of the background is obscured by the foreground image.

Although this occurs in a fraction of a second, it is likely that our eyes would catch this. In fact, the result would look pretty bad. If you could look back at some of the games made in the 1970s for the Apple II, you would notice that you can actually see the images as they are drawn.

What we do to get around this issue is to make use of two buffers. The buffer that displays the current image is called the *front buffer*. A second buffer (the *back buffer*) is a duplicate area of graphics memory in which we can add all the art assets, building up to a final image while the front buffer displays the previously rendered image. The back buffer is where we do all our work. When we're ready, we swap the front buffer with the back buffer. The result is that the user will see the image only when we're finished editing it.

In XNA, all we need to do is request that a back buffer be created at a specific size, and the framework will do the rest of the work for us.

```
public Game1()
{
  graphics = new GraphicsDeviceManager(this);
  graphics.PreferredBackBufferWidth = 1280;
  graphics.PreferredBackBufferHeight = 720;

  \\\...
}
```

In DirectX and OpenGL, this is only slightly more complicated because we explicitly tell the system when we want it to swap buffers.

2.4   Graphic File Formats

PNG files are the format of choice for most 2D games today, but it is worth taking a look at other common file formats.

2.4.1   Bitmap

Bitmap (BMP) files are the most basic of the image file formats. For all practical purposes, they simply store the raw image data as a 2D array of colors. For this reason, I use the term bitmap (lowercase B) throughout this book to refer to the generic concept of storing 2D pixel data in RAM (or video RAM).

The actual file format (Bitmap) has a few variations, but for the most part, it is a bit-for-bit match with the data in RAM. As a result, to process a bitmap file, all we need is the color depth and resolution of the image (stored in the file header).

This lack of compression means that the bitmap files can be processed very quickly. The downside is that they almost always require significantly more storage space than is necessary. As an example, consider the image part of the Taylor & Francis logo in Figure 2.17.

We can see that the image is composed of large amounts of white space, stored in a bitmap as a series of white pixels. In memory, a white pixel takes up just as much space as any other colored pixel, despite the fact that the white pixels are all the same.

With this in mind, a simple compression algorithm was developed that is ideal for logos or other images that contain groupings of pixels that are

Figure 2.17. Taylor & Francis logo (left) and a scaled version of it (right).

the same color. Instead of storing the same value for each pixel, we can group the pixels by color, storing the discrete number of that color. For example, instead of

$$FF\ 00\ 00,\ FF\ 00\ 00,\ FF\ 00\ 00,\ FF\ 00\ 00,\ FF\ FF\ FF,\ FF\ FF\ FF,$$

we can store the color of the pixel along with the number of occurrences before the pixel color changes:

$$FF\ 00\ 00\ (\times\ 4)\ FF\ FF\ FF\ (\times\ 2).$$

In so doing, we have dramatically decreased the storage requirements for the logo. This type of compression is called *run-length encoding*. It is simple to comprehend, and no data are lost during the compression process. An additional advantage is that the image can be created as the file is processed.

2.4.2   Graphics Interchange Format

The *graphics interchange format* (GIF) for images, developed in 1987, implements run-length encoding for compression as described above. This made GIF images an ideal choice for logos, and GIF was used extensively in the 1990s, especially on the web. Although GIF images can be used effectively to store an animation, GIF animations are more of a novelty and do not serve much use for game development.

Even worse, the GIF format has further strikes against it. First, the lossless compression algorithm used by the GIF format was patented by Unisys until 2004. Second, GIF images do not support transparency. Looking back at Figure 2.17 (right), we see that the edges of the image are a blend between white and blue. Now imagine that we wanted to place the image on a dark background. If the logo had a harder edge, we could open a graphics editor and simply replace all the white pixels with background color. But since the logo has a soft edge, the result is rather awful (see Figure 2.18).

Figure 2.18.   Taylor & Francis logo with a dark background.

Without the ability to store transparent pixels, the GIF file format is simply not robust enough for our needs.

2.4.3   Portable Network Graphics

Like GIF, the *portable network graphics* (PNG) file format supports lossless compression. It was developed in 1995 as a result of the two shortcomings of the GIF file type noted above (lack of support for transparency and patent issues). The PNG format is now the primary graphical storage format for 2D games.

2.4.4   Joint Photographic Experts Group

Unlike GIF and PNG, the *Joint Photographic Experts Group* (JPEG or JPG) image format utilizes lossy compression. That is, as the image is compressed, the original detail is lost and cannot be recovered.

The advantage of the JPEG format is that when used on photographs, it allows for a large compression ratio, as much as 10 to 1, with very little loss in compressed image quality. This makes JPEG a popular standard for photography and web pages. However, JPEG compression is not a good choice for 2D games. Not only is detail lost as an image is processed by JPEG compression, but more important, the format does not support transparency.

2.4.5   Truevision Advanced Raster Graphics Adapter

Developed as a native format for early graphics cards, Truevision graphics adapter (TGA) and Truevision advanced raster graphics adapter (TARGA) files allow for both raw and lossless compression. Simple in structure, TGA files were historically used for textures in 3D games.

2.4.6   XNA Binary

The last file type worth mentioning is XNA binary (XNB). XNA developers may notice that their PNG files are converted to XNB files. These binary files are created automatically during one of the final stages of the game deployment process by XNA Game Studio. They offer a minimal level of security so that raw PNGs won't be available to prying eyes. But, even though they are compressed into a Microsoft-specific format and protected by copyright, the images are not completely protected; exporters can be found on the Internet.

Exercises

Questions

2.1. Calculate the amount of memory (in bytes) to store a 1,024 × 768 24-bit RGB image.

2.1. At a garage sale, you find a used digital camera. On the side of the camera it states that it takes pictures that are 5.0 megapixels in size. What is a likely resolution (width and height) of the images taken by the camera. Assuming the images are in true color and stored uncompressed, how much space in memory does each image require?

2.1. Research a classic 2D game (one released prior to 1995). What was the resolution and color depth? What were other technical specs for the graphics hardware?

Challenges

Challenge 2.1. Write a program that allows the user to have complete control of the RGB color of the screen.

Here's some code to get you started:

1. Add a color member variable to the main game class:

```
public class Game1 : Microsoft.Xna.Framework.Game
{
    // ...
    Color backgroundColor = Color.Black;
    // ...
```

2. Add keyboard controls in the update function:

```
protected override void Update(GameTime gameTime)
{
    // ...
    if (Keyboard.GetState().IsKeyDown(Keys.Up))
        backgroundColor.R++;
    // ...
```

3. Use the member variable as the clear color in the Draw function:

```
protected override void Draw(GameTime gameTime)
{
    GraphicsDevice.Clear(backgroundColor);
    base.Draw(gameTime);
}
```

Challenge 2.2. Write a program that displays a chart of all the shades of gray in the 24-bit RGB color model by mapping a different color to each pixel.

To get you started, add the code below. For now, don't worry too much about the details of how the point sprite is created.

1. Add a tiny 1×1 sprite as a Texture2D member variable to the main game class:

```
1   public class Game1 : Microsoft.Xna.Framework.Game
    {
      // ...
      Texture2D pointSprite;
5     // ...
```

2. The following code will initialize the sprite. Add it to the Initialization function; we'll deal with the details of how it works later.

```
1   protected override void Initialize()
    {
      Color[] arrayOfColor = { Color.White };
      Rectangle pointRectangle = new Rectangle(0, 0, 1, 1);

5     pointSprite = new Texture2D(GraphicsDevice, 1, 1);
      pointSprite.SetData<Color>(0, pointRectangle,
          arrayOfColor, 0, 1);
```

3. Finally, the point sprite is drawn at a screen location and color as shown below in the Draw function.

```
1   protected override void Draw(GameTime gameTime)
    {
      GraphicsDevice.Clear(Color.Blue);

5     Vector2 myLocation = new Vector2(50, 50);
      Color myColor = Color.White;

      spriteBatch.Begin();

10    //Hint: create a loop of draw commands
      spriteBatch.Draw(pointSprite, myLocation, myColor);

      spriteBatch.End();

15    base.Draw(gameTime);
    }
```

Challenge 2.3. Write a program that displays a chart of all the colors in the 12-bit RGB color model by mapping a different color to each pixel.

Challenge 2.4. Write a program that allows the user to change the background color by using the hue-saturation-lightness (HSL) color palette.

Chapter 3
Sprites!

This chapter introduces the concept of a sprite and techniques for using them in games. It includes a discussion of sprite alphas and managing sprite depth, and it wraps up with a look at how multiple sprites are stored on a single *atlas*. The chapter also presents different approaches for ordering sprite sheets.

3.1 What Is a Sprite?

As mentioned in Section 2.1.1, a ***sprite*** is simply a bitmap image that we can use in our game. Very few images represent this as well as Tomohiro Nishikado's iconic space invader (Figure 3.1).

Figure 3.1. Sprite from *Space Invaders* (1978) [Nishikado 78].

These sprites can represent figures, such as Mario in the Nintendo series, or can be used to generate background, as was done in Origin's *Ultima* series. In the latter case, the term *tile graphics* might be used.

Richard Garriott attributes the invention of the tile graphic system he used in the *Ultima* series to his friend Ken Arnold. In Garriot's words,

> It's a little bit-mapped image ... thrown up on the screen that graphically represents what the world can look like. In the earliest days we actually had to draw those images on graph paper, convert those graphs to binary numbers ... convert those binary numbers into a stream of hex digits, enter those hex digits into the computer, and then try running the program and see what it looked like. [Garriott 90]

Of course, now we have much more sophisticated approaches to generating sprites, which I categorize into three approaches: raster based, vector based, and 3D based.

3.1.1   Raster-Based Sprite Generation

Raster-based sprite generation is only a step above the process that is described by Garriott above. The bitmapped images are created by an artist, pixel by pixel, in a graphics editor such as Adobe Photoshop. These editors might have very advanced features that help artists in their creative process, but the most important feature is that the artist is still working with individual pixels.

These types of graphics editors were the primary artists' tool through the early 1990s. Most 2D artists prefer vector editors, but a few artists still prefer building their images pixel by pixel, especially when working with very small sprites or wanting to create a large sprite with a retro look.

Additionally, even when the artist uses vector- or 3D-based tools, raster editors still play a role in the final editing of graphics. This is because the raster-based editors provide the pixel-level detail as well as a one-to-one relationship between what is created and what is rendered in the game.

3.1.2   Vector-Based Sprite Generation

Currently, *vector-based sprite* generation is more common with modern 2D games. The artist uses a graphics package such as Adobe Flash or Adobe Illustrator to draw vector graphics. Once the artwork is ready for the game, the vector graphics are exported through a process called *rasterization*, in which the artwork is converted into a pixel-based image. As Section 2.1.6 showed, vector graphics is more flexible and forgiving than pixel graphics, especially when it comes to rendering the same image at different scales.

3.1.3   3D-Based Sprite Generation

A third possibility for sprite generation is to create the image in 3D first, then take a snapshot of the rendered 3D image and save it as a bitmap. This was the process used in Rare's 1994 release of *Donkey Kong Country* for the Super NES and later for Blizzard Entertainment's 1996 *Diablo*.

Historically, *3D-based sprite* generation occurred as a result of an interesting gap in video game graphics when game developers were capable of generating game-quality 3D images, but most consumer hardware was not yet ready for the required graphics processing to render these images in real time. This technique is similar to vector-based sprite generation in that it allows the artist to work with a powerful toolset and still generate 2D raster graphics as a final product.

There has been a bit of a resurrection of 3D-based sprite generation recently as some game developers work to deploy the same 3D-quality images on mobile devices with lower processing power. This can be seen on recent releases of Sid Meier's *Civilization Revolution*, a 2D-tiled game enhanced with 3D-based sprites.

3.1.4 Sprite Sheets

For efficiency, multiple sprites are often grouped together in a single image file called a *sprite sheet*. An example is the user interface sprite sheet from *aliEnd* shown in Figure 3.2.

When it comes to drawing the sprite to the screen, we need to consider the three representations of the data:

1. **image file:** the compressed data as it exists in the file system (usually as a PNG image file);

2. **source data:** the bitmap loaded into memory along with any information needed to track the bitmap;

3. **destination data:** the information about where and how the individual sprite is drawn to the screen.

Figure 3.2. User interface sprite sheet for *aliEnd*.

3.1.5   Textures and Loading Content

We have already examined file types in Chapter 2 and PNG is the best choice for our needs. The companion website to this book, http://www. 2dGraphicsProgramming.com, contains the art assets used in the examples. The first of these is snow_assets.png, described next.

In XNA, we will need to add an instance of the Texture2D class to the game class, then load the bitmap data from the file system into Texture2D during the content load phase:

```
public class Game1 : Microsoft.Xna.Framework.Game
{
    GraphicsDeviceManager graphics;
    SpriteBatch spriteBatch;

    Texture2D snowSpriteTexture;  // Add a Texture2D sprite

//...
```

```
protected override void LoadContent()
{
    spriteBatch = new SpriteBatch(GraphicsDevice);

    snowSpriteTexture = Content.Load<Texture2D>("snow_assets"
        ); // Load the image "snow_assets.png"

//...
```

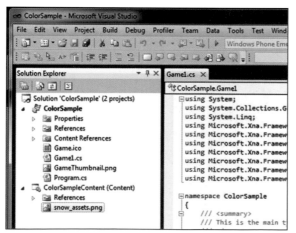

Figure 3.3. PNG file added to the content folder in Solution Explorer.

You now will need to add the image file (in this case, snow_assets.png) to the project into the content folder. In Visual C# Express you will take the following steps. When you are done, you should see something similar to Figure 3.3.

1. **Locate your Content project:** The Solution Explorer lists two projects; the first is for your game code and the second is for your game content, labeled (Content).

2. **Add the file snow_assets.png:** Right click on the content project and select Add → Existing Item. Find the file and click the Add button.

3.1.6   Source Data versus Destination Data

Now that we have the sprite file uncompressed and stored in memory, we can draw it to the screen. Common practice is to group all the sprite draw requests together in a series. XNA provides a class (SpriteBatch) for just that purpose.

To draw a sprite to the screen, at a minimum we need to pass the source texture (Texture2D), the destination location (a point on the screen), and the color (usually Color.White). We can use the XNA type Vector2 to store the location.

```
protected override void Draw(GameTime gameTime)
{
  GraphicsDevice.Clear(Color.CornflowerBlue);

  Vector2 myLocation = new Vector2(50, 50);
  Color myColor = Color.White;

  spriteBatch.Begin();

  //Hint: create a loop of draw commands
  spriteBatch.Draw(snowSpriteTexture, myLocation, myColor);
    // Minimum parameters needed: Texture2D, Vector2, Color

  spriteBatch.End();

  base.Draw(gameTime);
}
```

With this code, we draw the entire sprite sheet to the screen (see Figure 3.4) with the top-left corner of the sprite texture located at $x = 50$, $y = 50$. This simple example has a few interesting properties.

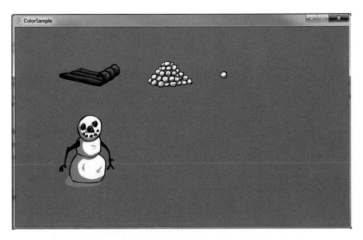

Figure 3.4. Sprite sheet example.

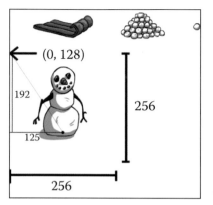

Figure 3.5. Values for the location, origin, and width/height of snowman sprite on the sprite sheet.

First, notice that the size of the original texture is 512 texels wide by 512 texels high, and the entire texture is drawn to the screen. This is not something we commonly would do in practice. In most cases, we want to draw only a part of the stored bitmap (an individual sprite). To do this we'll track the rectangular location of the sprite on the sprite sheet. In Figure 3.5, we define a 256-pixel square box around the snowman at location $(0, 128)$ representing the snowman sprite. Similarly, the sled is located at position $(0, 0)$ but has a width of 256 and a height of 128. The location of all sprites on the sprite sheet will need to be tracked. We call this information *source data*.

Second, notice that there is a 1:1 ratio between texels and pixels. This doesn't have to be the case. When drawing the sprite, we have the option of scaling the image. We talk more about scaling in Section 3.4.

Third, the colors of the pixels on the screen are an exact match to the colors that were in the original image file. This also does not have to be the case. By applying any color other than white to the Draw call, we can tint the sprite as it appears on the screen. A shade of gray that changes over time could be used to implement a fade-in effect, or perhaps the color red can indicate that the sprite is damaged.

Any information related to the way the sprite is drawn to the screen we call *destination data*, and we track it separately from the source data. We keep them separate because there is not necessarily a one-to-one relationship between sprites on the sprite sheet and those on the screen. For example, we may want to draw two snowmen, in which case the source data will be the same for both, but the destination data will be different.

XNA Sprite Source Data		**XNA Sprite Destination Data**	
	Data Type		Data Type
bitmap	Texture2D	screen location and scale	Vector2 and float
location	Rectangle	*or* destination rectangle	Rectangle
origin	Vector2	rotation	float
		color	RGBA color
		depth	float
		effects	SpriteEffects

In addition to the bitmap and location, it is also useful to take note of the sprite origin. By default, the origin is in the upper-left corner of the sprite $(0,0)$. The origin is relative to the x-y location coordinates. When a sprite is rotated, the rotation occurs around the origin (see Figure 3.6).

Figure 3.6. Sprite drawn and rotated around default origin (left), and the same sprite drawn and rotated around an origin defined at the center of the sprite (right).

3.1.7   Sample Program: A Moving Sprite with Alpha

In the following example, we'll draw two snowmen. The first will be drawn normally at a fixed location. For the second, we'll allow the player to move.

First, we'll need to add variables to store the source and destination data:

```
public class Game1 : Microsoft.Xna.Framework.Game
{
  GraphicsDeviceManager graphics;
  SpriteBatch spriteBatch;

  //Sprite Source Data
  Texture2D snowAssetTexture;
  Rectangle snowmanSourceLocation;

  //Sprite Destination Data
  Vector2 firstSnowmanLocation;
  Vector2 secondSnowmanLocation;
  Vector2 secondSnowmanOrigin;
  Color secondSnowmanColor;
  float secondSnowmanScale;
  float secondSnowmanRotation;
  //...
```

During the initialization phase, we'll define the destination locations. Initialization can also be a good place to set our resolution, so we'll add that here as well.

```
protected override void Initialize()
{
  firstSnowmanLocation = new Vector2(200,500);
```

```
 5    secondSnowmanLocation = new Vector2(400, 500);
      secondSnowmanRotation = 0.0f;
      secondSnowmanColor = Color.Plum;
      secondSnowmanScale = 0.5f;

10    //Set HD Resolution with a 9:16 aspect ratio
      graphics.PreferredBackBufferWidth = 1280;
      graphics.PreferredBackBufferHeight = 720;
      graphics.ApplyChanges();
      //...
```

In the content loading phase, we'll set the details for the source data.

```
 1  protected override void LoadContent()
    {
      spriteBatch = new SpriteBatch(GraphicsDevice);

 5    snowAssetTexture = Content.Load<Texture2D>("snow_assets");
      snowmanSourceLocation = new Rectangle(0, 128, 256, 256);
      snowmanSourceOrigin = new Vector2(128, 192);
    }
```

In the update loop, we'll allow the player to modify the position of the second snowman by using the left and right arrow keys.

```
 1  protected override void Update(GameTime gameTime)
    {
      // Allows the game to exit
      if (GamePad.GetState(PlayerIndex.One).Buttons.Back ==
          ButtonState.Pressed)
 5        this.Exit();

      if (Keyboard.GetState().IsKeyDown(Keys.Left))
          secondSnowmanLocation.X--;
      if (Keyboard.GetState().IsKeyDown(Keys.Right))
10        secondSnowmanLocation.X++;

      base.Update(gameTime);
    }
```

Finally, in the Draw loop, we'll draw the two snowmen. Figure 3.7 shows a sample of the output.

```
 1  protected override void Draw(GameTime gameTime)
    {
      GraphicsDevice.Clear(Color.White);

 5    spriteBatch.Begin();
      spriteBatch.Draw(snowAssetTexture,
              firstSnowmanLocation,
              snowmanSourceLocation,
              Color.White,              // Color
10            0.0f,                     // Rotation
```

```
                    snowmanSourceOrigin,
                    1.0f,                    // Scale
                    SpriteEffects.None,      // Flip sprite?
                    1.0f);                   // Depth
15     spriteBatch.Draw(snowAssetTexture,
                    secondSnowmanLocation,
                    snowmanSourceLocation,
                    secondSnowmanColor,
                    secondSnowmanRotation,
20                  snowmanSourceOrigin,
                    secondSnowmanScale,
                    SpriteEffects.None,      //Flip sprite?
                    0.5f);                   //Depth
       spriteBatch.End();
25
       base.Draw(gameTime);
    }
```

Figure 3.7. Sample output from "Moving Sprite with Alpha."

3.2 Layering with Depth

You may have noticed in the previous example (Figure 3.7) that the smaller snowman is in front of the larger one. This is simply because the smaller snowman was drawn after the larger snowman.

You may have also noticed a depth value in the Draw call. The depth value allows you to place the sprites on layers (any float value between 0 and 1). By default, the depth value is ignored. The Draw calls are placed in a queue, and then when `SpriteBatch.End()` is called, the sprites are drawn to the screen. However, by setting the sort mode in `SpriteBatch.Begin()`, you have access to some very useful options. Simply replace

```
1   spriteBatch.Begin();
```

with

```
1   spriteBatch.Begin(SpriteSortMode.BackToFront, BlendState.
        AlphaBlend);
```

In `BackToFront`, the sprites are sorted by the depth value so that the greater values are drawn last. For the reverse, just use the sort mode `FrontToBack`.

Now imagine a game that involves a tiled surface consisting of randomly generated sprites from various sprite sheets. On sprite sheet A are sprites 1–9, and on sprite sheet B are sprites 10–19. In the game, you loop through the tiled background 1, 17, 4, 15, 6, 6, 11, and so on.

When it comes time to draw the sprites, it would be much more efficient to draw all the sprites from sheet A and then all the sprites from sheet B (instead of switching back and forth from A to B in the order that was provided). In this case (where layering does not matter because none of the sprites will overlap), choose the sort mode Texture. The system will automatically order the sprites in the most efficient order before drawing them.

3.2.1 Tracking Depth

There may be other times that we may want to change the layering of the sprites based on in-game conditions. As an example, in the snowmen program we could give the appearance of depth by using the y-value to control the drawing order, so the closer the sprite is to the top of the screen, the farther away it is. The faraway sprites are drawn first, so they are overlapped by the closer sprites.

To track depth in the snowman example, first you'll need to ensure the sprite batch is set to use `FrontToBack` sprite sorting, as shown in the previous code snippet.

You'll also need to allow the player to change the y-value of the sprite by adding the up and down input to the update function:

```
1   if (Keyboard.GetState().IsKeyDown(Keys.Up))
        secondSnowmanLocation.Y--;
    if (Keyboard.GetState().IsKeyDown(Keys.Down))
        secondSnowmanLocation.Y++;
```

Finally, you'll need to add a depth calculation for the sprites. Since we need a value between 0 and 1, we can simply divide the y-coordinate of the sprite's location by the screen height. In our case,

$$\text{depth} = \frac{\text{sprite's destination } y\text{-value}}{\text{screen height}}.$$

In code, this would be

```
1   spriteBatch.Draw(snowAssetTexture,
                     firstSnowmanLocation,
                     snowmanSourceLocation,
                     Color.White,
5                    0.0f,
                     snowmanSourceOrigin,
                     1.0f,
                     SpriteEffects.None,
                     firstSnowmanLocation.Y/720.0f); //depth
                         calculated
10  spriteBatch.Draw(snowAssetTexture,
                     secondSnowmanLocation,
                     snowmanSourceLocation,
                     secondSnowmanColor,
                     secondSnowmanRotation,
15                   snowmanSourceOrigin,
                     secondSnowmanScale,
                     SpriteEffects.None,
```

```
secondSnowmanLocation.Y / 720.0f); //depth
            calculated
```

Using the sprite's height to give the illusion of depth is a common technique in games. We'll go into much greater detail about this and other ways to create the illusion of depth in Chapter 6.

3.3   The Sprite Sheet and the GPU

Before we discuss the details of the sprite sheet, it is important to go into a little detail about computer hardware. Most modern computers and game consoles have at least two processors: the *CPU* and a separate *GPU*. The GPU is a separate processor dedicated to graphics processing. Unless you're playing a computer game or some other 3D simulation, the GPU is mostly idle, waiting for you to send it some graphics to process.

3.3.1   The Power of Two

You may have heard someone in graphics say, "The image needs to be a power of two." The *power of two* refers to a requirement that the textures on the graphics card must have width and height values that are equivalent to 2^n where n is any number. In other words, width and height have values of 1, 2, 4, 8, 16, 32, 64, 128, 256, 512, 1,024, 2,048, 4,096, 8,192, etc.

Actually, the "etc." isn't really needed because most graphics cards can't handle larger textures (at least for now). In fact, most systems can accept textures up to only 2,048 × 2,048. The following chart shows some current texture limitations.

System	Texture Capacity	Storage Size
iPad		
Most PC graphics cards	2048^2 at 32 bpp	16,777,216 bytes
iPad retina		
PlayStation 3		
Many PC graphics cards	4096^2 at 32 bpp	67,108,864 bytes
Xbox 360	8192^2 at 32 bpp	268,435,456 bytes

Even though there are some exceptions, it's important to keep your textures as powers of two. Many of the functions within the graphics package require power of two textures. In XNA, this is true for any of the "wrapping" sampler states.

In going through some old emails, I actually found the following warning, which was broadcast to the whole company by a clearly frustrated graphics programmer. I'm sure he won't mind if I reprint it here:

Everyone probably knows this, but just for sanities sake.

All textures *must* have dimensions that are a multiple of 4. Power of 2 dimensions are preferred for in-game textures.

If anyone checks in a texture with a screwy size, a hot mug of tea will be thrown in your direction at speed.

Thank you for your cooperation.

3.3.2   Textures and Graphics Hardware

When you use the XNA content pipeline (`Content.Load()`), you're copying the data from the file system and storing it onto the graphics card. The graphics card contains both the GPU and some memory needed to store your texture data.

The graphics card performs best when the textures are a power of two. Then it doesn't need to do any conversion to your texture data to fit it into memory. (Modern hardware will automatically pad your texture to be a power of two.)

This is one of the reasons you'll often see multiple sprites on a single sprite sheet instead of having them managed as individual textures. The goal is to pack the sprites so that the final sprite sheet texture is a power of two.

However, as we discussed earlier, the fact that there are multiple sprites on a single texture means you have an added overhead of tracking the location and size of the sprites on the sprite sheet. In addition, you can't just pack the sprites as closely as possible. Instead, you have to ensure there is enough white space around each sprite so that the rectangular representation of one sprite does not include bits of the others.

3.3.3   Structured Sprite Sheets

An easy way to build your sprite sheets is to simply divide your texture into equal-size spaces. Referring to Section 3.2, it is easy to see how this might be done. It also makes it easy to programmatically loop through the sprites. This is convenient (in fact, I'll use this for some examples in Chapter 4), but there are a few disadvantages to this approach.

First, it can lead to some wasted space. Each sprite is not packed as tightly as it could be on the sprite sheet because it must fit nicely into the predefined box size.

Second, it is unlikely that your artist will work within the sprite sheet for editing. Creating the sprite sheet is usually a last step, and if the individual sprites need to be modified later, the sprite sheet will need to be recreated.

Third, the sprite sheet does not include any information about the number of sprites, the sprites' locations, or their origins. All of that information must be tracked separately.

3.3.4 Generated Sprite Atlas

As previously mentioned, it is quite likely that your artist's favorite drawing software does not generate nicely structured sprite sheets. In fact, it is possible that your artist may not even know about the power of two issue (or consider it your problem alone).

As an example, when working on the artwork for *aliEnd*, the artist would draw in Adobe Flash and then export the animated cels using an exporter built into Flash. (We'll take a closer look at animated cels in Chapter 4.) The resultant output of the Flash sprite exporter is a series of individual PNG files, one for each frame of the animation.

Here is where your software pipeline can come to the rescue. With the help of a software tool (e.g., Andreas Löw's TexturePacker), you can automatically trim, rotate, and create an efficiently packed and sized sprite sheet along with an associated text file containing the location and orientation of all the sprites in the texture. This type of sprite sheet, which includes a text file with location information, is often referred to as a *sprite atlas*.

3.4   Scaling Sprites

We have briefly discussed the concept of scaling sprites; however, I encourage you to scale sprites with caution. Generally, by maintaining a one-to-one relationship between the pixels created by the artist on a sprite sheet and the pixels as they appear on screen, you are guaranteed the best quality (and a happy artist).

With that said, it may be necessary at times to scale an image (we'll look at a case sample in Chapter 6). When this happens, you generally want to scale down instead of scaling up.

3.4.1   Sampler State

Any time you scale an image, there is no longer a one-to-one relationship between the pixels in your sprite and the pixels on the screen. In fact, it is fairly easy to imagine that an up-scaled sprite will look pixelated. However, there are issues with down-scaling an image as well.

Consider the simple example shown in Figure 3.8. If you scale a 4×4 sprite to 2×2 screen pixels, what color should be placed in each pixel?

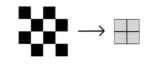

Figure 3.8. Scaling a 16-texel sprite texture down to four-screen pixels.

Figure 3.9. Three snowmen, left to right: original scale, nearest-neighbor doubled, and linear doubled.

As you can see, there is not an easy answer. Admittedly, this is an extreme case, but it illustrates the problem of down-scaling.

Most graphics packages offer at least two types of scaling options, called *scaling filters* or *sampler types*. *Scaling filters* determine which texel on the original sprite will be the sample used to color the corresponding pixel. Common types are nearest neighbor, linear, bilinear, and bicubic.

The two latter types are costly in processing time and more useful for 3D graphics or photo-realistic applications. For 2D games, the choice is simpler: when scaling an image, do you want to preserve the specific texel color (creating a more pixelated image while preserving hard edges and original colors) or are you willing to render an averaged color (creating a smoother image but losing the precision).

Figure 3.9 illustrates the difference between nearest-neighbor and linear filtering. (Note that the middle figure is more pixelated but retains better color quality when compared to the figure on the right.) In XNA, our options are available when creating the sprite batch. Just as we defined a sprite sort method in the Begin call, we can also define a sampler state. In XNA our options are `SamplerState.PointClamp` for nearest-neighbor filtering and `SamplerState.LinearClamp` for linear filtering.

In addition, graphics filters may offer the choice of clamping or wrapping. These options are used when determining what to do with edge cases.

3.4.2   Mipmapping

Although beyond the scope of this text, it is worth knowing about *mipmapping*, a really useful GPU hardware functionality in which the textures are prescaled and placed on a single texture. If the original texture is 256^2 in size, the subsequent down-scaled images are each half-sized, resulting in a series of images that are 128^2, 64^2, 32^2, 16^2, 8^2, 4^2, 2^2, and 1^2 in size (see Figure 3.10).

The result is an increase of only one-third in storage space with great advantages. This is because instead of scaling a very large image at runtime, which might create significantly blurry or pixelated results, the prescaled images can be used. Normally, this technique is used in 3D graphics to improve the quality of distant (down-scaled) textures.

However, if generated manually (instead of allowing the GPU to do the mipmapping automatically), the artist can see and edit the resultant scaled images. This allows the artist to have significantly greater control of

Figure 3.10. Mipmapped texture.

the final quality of the graphics if your game uses large amounts of scaled sprites.

3.4.3 Scaling the Batch

Finally, note that XNA offers the ability to scale the entire sprite batch. This is really useful if you need to automatically resize your game scene for different resolutions.

When developing for mobile devices, I tend to render the initial scene at 1,280 × 720, then apply a scaled matrix to the entire sprite batch based on the ratio between the default resolution and the device resolution. For example, the Kindle Fire has a resolution of 1,024 × 600. The result is a screen width scaled down to 0.8 the original size.

By using code such as the following, you will be able to render to various screen resolutions without much effort.

```
Matrix scaledMatrix = Matrix.CreateScale(actualScreenSize.
    Width/defaultScreenSize.Width);
spriteBatch.Begin(,,,,,, scaledMatrix);
```

Be aware, however, that, as with other types of scaling, this works only to a limit. Rendering an image three times larger or smaller than the original is going to result in a fairly poor quality final image. An actual example of this appears in Section 5.2.

Exercises

Questions

3.1. What is the smallest power of two texture that will fit one of each of the following sized sprites: 1,024 × 1,024, 512 × 512, 256 × 256, 128 × 128, 64 × 64, 32 × 32, 16 × 16, 8 × 8, 4 × 4, 2 × 2, and 1 × 1?

3.1. Research a classic arcade system or game console (released prior to 2000). What was the maximum texture size? By including the system's color depth, calculate the amount of memory required to store the maximum-size texture for that system.

Challenges

Challenge 3.1. The act of repeating a simple shape in various orientations has been used throughout history. Great examples can be found by searching the Internet for images of quilt patterns, tiled floors, and various stonework. Your challenge is to create a tiled pattern using just one or two sprites.

As an example, Figure 3.11 shows an output created from a single sprite, repeated, rotated, and colored via a loop within the sprite batch Draw call.

Figure 3.11. Sample patterns from repeating a single sprite.

Challenge 3.2. In the sample code we have worked through so far, the source and destination data associated with each sprite have been stored in individual variables. Your challenge is to create a more robust code architecture to store and render multiple sprites on multiple sprite sheets.

A good place to start is with an object-oriented architecture. A sprite class could include a reference to the texture as well as sprite source data. An object class could include a reference to the sprite class as well as the appropriate destination data.

Challenge 3.3. Create a process for parsing the data in a sprite atlas. Your project should read in both the image file and the corresponding text file as generated by software such as TexturePackerPro.

Part II

Motion and Depth

Chapter 4

Animation

So far we have covered the basic task of getting a sprite to appear on the screen. As such, the code samples in the preceding chapters were necessarily focused on a specific graphics library (OpenGL, DirectX, XNA). Going forward, we will focus less on the specifics of the language and more on building structures that are not platform specific.

In this chapter we start by looking at the basics of sprite animation, dealing with timing issues to ensure the animation works independent of frame rate. We also look at the broader topic of animation outside of the game industry and what we can learn from the animation pioneers of the twentieth century.

4.1 Historical Animation

Animation comes from the Latin word *animatus*, meaning "to give life" or "to live." The process through which an animator gives life is through a knowledge of form and movement combined with various animation techniques and finally topped off with a considerable amount of patience and artistic sensibility.

The most successful early film animators were the ones who understood that animation is more than the mechanics of a walking sequence. The ability of a talented artist to breathe life into a drawing can be accomplished even without the help of the animated sequence. The mid-nineteenth century artist Honoré Daumier is known for his ability to do just that, and he was often referenced as an example by early film animators [Thomas and Johnston 81]. A wonderful example of the sense of animation in Daumier's work is shown in Figure 4.1.

Figure 4.1. Breathing life into art: *NADAR élevant la Photographie à la hauteur de l'Art* (*NADAR elevating Photography to Art*) by Honoré Daumier (lithograph, 1863).

It is for this life-giving ability that we turn to our game artists and animators. However, as programmers working closely with animators, we may be able to augment their work by providing a technology-based set of tools to help with the mechanics of animation. This is especially important when we take into account the interactive nature of game animation.

In traditional animation, the artist had full control of every object location and velocity across the scene for every frame in the sequence. The game animator must give up that control, however, in order to allow players to feel that they are driving the actions of the game. The player may want to dive to the right or fire a missile to the left midway through the walk cycle. This is where the graphics programmer comes in, as a conduit linking the artist with the player. The programmer must understand the mechanics of the game as well as the mechanics of animation.

4.2   Cel Animation

The term *cel*, short for *celluloid*, refers to the transparent sheet used by film animators to draw images that would later be placed on top of a generally static background and photographed as an individual frame on film. We borrow the term here, as it is the same conceptual process we use when animating sprites.

This concept of looping through a set of sprites to create the animated sequence is fairly simple. To implement it, we need to plan the following steps:

- **Add code to track the animation sequence:** This means we need to know the total number of cels, the current cel being displayed, the amount of time each cel should be displayed, and the current time that has elapsed.

- **Loop through the animation:** In the update function, we need to add the logic for checking how much time has elapsed and for incrementing the cel counter appropriately when it is time to move to the next frame in the animation.

- **Render the appropriate frame from the sprite sheet:** In our case, the cels are evenly spaced on a structured sprite sheet such that the first cel is at position $(0,0)$, the second cel is at position $(width, 0)$, the next at $(width \times 2, 0)$, and so on. This type of structured sprite sheet makes it very easy to loop through the sprite cels without any significant overhead (not necessarily the robust solution we would want in a full game, but it does allow us to see the animation working very quickly).

Starting with an XNA game template, all we need to do is add the following code snippets. As before, the sprite sheets we use in this example can be found on the companion website, http://www.2dGraphicsProgramming. com.

So, we add the following member variables to the game class:

```
1    //Source Data
     private Texture2D    runCycleTexture;
     private Rectangle    currentCelLocation;

5    //Destination Data
     private Vector2      runnerPosition;

     //Animation Data
     private int          currentCel;
10   private int          numberOfCels;

     private int          msUntilNextCel;    //in milliseconds
     private int          msPerCel;          //in milliseconds
```

The value `msPerCel` is a measure of how many milliseconds are required for each frame of the animation. For example, if your animation requires a frame rate of 20 frames per second, milliseconds per cell would be calculated as

$$\frac{\text{seconds}}{20 \text{ frames}} \times \frac{1,000 \text{ milliseconds}}{\text{second}} = 50 \frac{\text{milliseconds}}{\text{frame}}.$$

We then use this value in our initialization, along with the total number of cels and the rectangular coordinates for the first cel on the sprite sheet.

Notice that the sprite width and height are constant. We'll use these values when later calculating the position on the sprite sheet for the current cel in the animation.

```
1        numberOfCels = 12;
         currentCel = 0;

         msPerCel = 50;
5        msUntilNextCel = msPerCel;

         currentCelLocation.X = 0;
         currentCelLocation.Y = 0;
         currentCelLocation.Width = 128;     //sprite width
10       currentCelLocation.Height = 128;    //sprite height

         runnerPosition = new Vector2(100, 100);
```

Loading the content is the same as before, now with our animated sprite sheet:

```
1    runCycleTexture = Content.Load<Texture2D>("run_cycle");
```

A common mistake for novice programmers is to simply increment to the next cel for each frame, but we'll take a better approach. In the Update function, we will subtract the number of elapsed milliseconds from our `msUntilNextCel` counter. For a fixed frame rate of 60 fps on the Xbox 360, this would be about 16.7 ms. On a mobile device running at 30 fps, this would be about 23 ms. Then, once the `msUntilNextCel` counter reaches zero, we'll move to the next cel and reset the `msUntilNextCel` counter to the value in `msPerCel`.

Using the elapsed time (instead of simply incrementing the cel counter every frame) allows us an animation architecture that is more platform independent. It ensures that the animation will react correctly to inconsistencies in the frame rate at runtime.

This demonstrates an important game programming paradigm. You should always ensure your code reacts as expected to variations in processor speed. Early game programmers learned this the hard way. You may have had the experience yourself when playing an old game on a modern PC and finding that the animation sequences occur faster than originally intended.

```
msUntilNextCel -= gameTime.ElapsedGameTime.Milliseconds;

if (msUntilNextCel <= 0)
  {
      currentCel++;
      msUntilNextCel = msPerCel;
  }

if (currentCel >= numberOfCels)
  currentCel = 0;

currentCelLocation.X = currentCelLocation.Width * currentCel;
```

The last line in the above code is the key to the structured sprite sheet. As Figure 4.2 shows, all the cels are structured along a single line in the sprite sheet. The result is that for each sprite in the animation sequence, the height, width, and y-value all remain constant. The only variation is the x-value, and it is simply a product of the cel width and `currentCel`. If you ever wondered why programmers like to count from 0 to 9 instead of from 1 to 10, this is a great visualization of the advantages.

Finally, we add our Draw call into the sprite batch.

```
    spriteBatch.Begin();
    spriteBatch.Draw( runCycleTexture,
                      runnerPosition,
                      currentCelLocation,
                      Color.White );
    spriteBatch.End();
```

Figure 4.2. Run cycle sprite sheet.

4.3   A Few Principles of Animation

4.3.1   Timing

Now that we've looked at implementing animation for a sequence using 50 ms per cel, why don't we just render all the animations at a constant frame rate? After all, if the game runs at 60 fps, shouldn't the animations also run at 60 fps?

Actually, not only is 60 fps far higher than needed to see clear animations, it is also a bit much to ask of your animator. The actual frame rate for an animated sprite is going to be based on two factors:

1. How fast is the object moving?

2. How big is the object?

Smaller and slower-moving objects will require a lower fps than larger, fast objects for smooth-looking movement. What this really comes down to is a question of establishing an ideal ratio between the *pixel delta* and the frame time. When there is a greater variance in pixels per frame, the animation will be less smooth. When the pixel delta is relatively small (say, 5 pixels:50 ms), it's easy for your brain to fill in the gaps of what should happen between each frame. However, as the pixel:time ratio is increased, there will come a point at which your brain is unable to fill in the gap (at, say, 50 pixels:50 ms). Conversely, if your pixel:time ratio is too small (5 pixels:500 ms), your brain will be waiting for motion when none is occurring.

This may be a bit hard to grasp without seeing an example, so one is provided on the companion website, http://www.2dGraphicsProgramming. com.

The results of my personal (rather unscientific) testing can be seen in Figure 4.3, which shows the results of running a 64 × 64 sprite across a 1,280 × 720 screen at various pixel deltas and frame rates. The green area shows the minimum number of frames per second (maximum milliseconds per frame) that are needed to prevent the moving image from seeming to stutter. The yellow area shows where the pixel delta is so great for that frame rate that it starts to create a blurring of the image. The red area shows where the blurring becomes so extreme that it appears there are two images.

In my testing, the fps rate was topped at 60 fps, thanks to the XNA framework and my monitor's refresh rate. The results also may vary based on the monitor's pixel density.

The point of this slight distraction is to show that your artist may provide various speeds for different animated clips. For example, a character

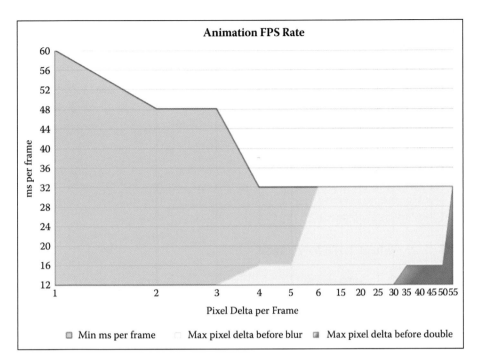

Figure 4.3. Graph of animation fps rate.

in the foreground with lots of detail may have a greater frame rate than some small background animation. Whatever the rates, it's important to work with the artist to ensure that the final look matches what is expected. Building in the flexibility for a modifiable `msPerCel` gives your artist a value that can later be tweaked.

It also is important to ensure that the sprite's movement speed across the game world matches the frame rate. If you are too fast or too slow, it will be obvious. (I suppose if you ran the animation in reverse you would get a moonwalk effect.)

I'm obviously not the first to experiment with animation timing. In 1981, Disney animators Ollie Johnston and Frank Thomas released a book, *The Illusion of Life* [Thomas and Johnston 81], detailing their experiences working in animation since the 1930s. The authors describe the 12 basic principles of animation, including the importance of timing.

Of the 12 principles, most are more relevant to the game artist than to the graphics programmer. They deal with such concepts as creating anticipation, exaggerating, ensuring the animated figure looks solid (as opposed to a two-dimensional drawing), and giving the animated character charm.

However, including timing, four of the principles of animation are worth looking more closely at to see how a bit of code might help the artist achieve the same goals:

1. timing,

2. slow in/slow out,

3. arcs,

4. follow-through and overlapping action.

Just as with the principle of timing, there may be a role for the graphics programmer to create a system that will allow the artist to harness the power of the processor to do some of the work.

4.3.2   Slow In/Slow Out

Figure 4.4. Animation principle: slow in/slow out.

Put simply, the principle of *slow in/slow out* (Figure 4.4) is just the concept of acceleration as applied to animation. In the discussion of timing, we identified that the artist will set a frame rate for the animated sequence. But if we start at the full animation rate, it doesn't look natural.

Let's try the following additions to our earlier animation code. First, we add a flag to track whether the player is running and `SpriteEffects` so that we can flip the sprite when he runs in the other direction. Add these to the other game class member variables:

```
private bool bIsRunning;
private SpriteEffects eRunnerSprEff;
```

Then we add initialization for the sprite effect:

```
eRunnerSprEff = SpriteEffects.None;
```

In the game update, we add keyboard input and a check of the `bIsRunning` flag before incrementing `currentCel`:

```
\\...

bIsRunning = false;

if (Keyboard.GetState().IsKeyDown(Keys.Left))
{
    bIsRunning = true;
    runnerPosition.X--;
    eRunnerSprEff = SpriteEffects.FlipHorizontally;
}
```

```
     else if (Keyboard.GetState().IsKeyDown(Keys.Right))
     {
         bIsRunning = true;
         runnerPosition.X++;
15       eRunnerSprEff = SpriteEffects.None;
     }


     if ((msUntilNextCel <= 0) && (bIsRunning))
20   {
         currentCel++;
         msUntilNextCel = msPerCel;
     }

25   \\...
```

As a last step, we replace the Draw call with one that includes the sprite Effect call.

```
1    spriteBatch.Begin();
     spriteBatch.Draw(runCycleTexture,
                     runnerPosition,
                     currentCelLocation,
5                    Color.White,
                     0.0f,            //Rotation
                     Vector2.Zero,    //Origin
                     1.0f,            //scale
                     eRunnerSprEff,
10                   1.0f);
     spriteBatch.End();
```

The result should be an animated character that suffers from the lack of slow in/slow out.

What we need to do now is to add in our understanding of this animation principle. First, we use acceleration to get the runner up to speed and add a dampening value to slow the runner once the player is no longer pressing the movement key. So, we add Game member values (runnerVelocity and maxRunnerVelocity)

```
1        private Vector2 runnerVelocity;
         private Vector2 maxRunnerVelocity;
```

and initialize

```
1        runnerVelocity = new Vector2(0, 0);
         maxRunnerVelocity = new Vector2(5, 0);
```

Then, in our update, we need to replace the previous keyboard input with one that will handle the new velocity variables:

```
1        if (Keyboard.GetState().IsKeyDown(Keys.Left))
         {
```

```
             if (runnerVelocity.X > -maxRunnerVelocity.X)
                 runnerVelocity.X -= 0.2f;
  5          eRunnerSprEff = SpriteEffects.FlipHorizontally;
         }
         else if (Keyboard.GetState().IsKeyDown(Keys.Right))
         {
             if (runnerVelocity.X < maxRunnerVelocity.X)
 10              runnerVelocity.X += 0.2f;
             eRunnerSprEff = SpriteEffects.None;
         }
         else
         {
 15          runnerVelocity *= 0.95f;
         }

         runnerPosition += runnerVelocity;
```

Now we need a way to tie the `msPerCel` to the player's speed. In this next bit of code, we do a couple of different things. First, we assume that the shortest `msUntilNextCel` is the value previously defined in `msPerCel` and the highest `msUntilNextCel` is twice that value. We then modify the value we assign to `msUntilNextCel` based on the relative velocity.

The relative velocity, determined as a percentage of the maximum velocity, is then used in determining the milliseconds until the next cel:

$$\texttt{msUntilNextCel} = \texttt{msPerCel} \times \left(1.0 + \left(1.0 - \frac{\text{current velocity}}{\text{maximum velocity}}\right)\right).$$

This will work as long as the runner is moving, but the moment the runner stops, you want the animation to stop as well. In that case, we simply calculate the relative velocity a bit earlier and use it as the conditional flag instead of our previous `isRunning` flag.

```
  1  float relativeVelocity = Math.Abs(runnerVelocity.X /
         maxRunnerVelocity.X);

     if (relativeVelocity > 0.05f)
     {
  5      if (msUntilNextCel <= 0)
         {
             currentCel++;
             msUntilNextCel = (int)(msPerCel * (2.0f -
                 relativeVelocity));
 10      }
     }
```

This works fairly well and you should be able to see a nice acceleration effect on the runner and associated animation, as demonstrated in Figure 4.4.

It is important to point out that this is a fairly simple example and it is not necessarily how you would want to do it in a production environment.

There are two issues:

1. The calculation of milliseconds is only indirectly tied to the velocity. The velocity changes, but we don't update the milliseconds until the previous millisecond counter expires and we are moving to the next frame. If the previous `msUntilNextCel` time was long and then we suddenly sped up, we could end up with an animation that is slow to respond (we would have to wait until the `msUntilNextCel` value reached zero before we take into account the higher velocity). We might have better luck with hooking the velocity directly into the `msUntilNextCel`. Such an approach will be a slightly more complicated solution, but should it produce a more responsive result.

2. The other, perhaps more important issue is the use of magic numbers throughout the sample. You may find that tinkering with the values and thresholds (there were references to 50, 5, 0.2, 0.05, and 0.95) allows for a better effect. But by hard coding these values into the program, the artists and designers will be unable to edit them. Ideally, these values should be something that you could edit at runtime (to see the immediate effect of changes). Even better, allow them to be saved into a configuration file during testing. (Obviously this is a feature you would turn off before releasing your game.)

The exact nature of your slow in/slow out solution will be up to you and your artist and should be based on the type of art assets with which you are working.

4.3.3 Arcs

The principle of *arcs* simply states that things in the real world tend to move in arcs (Figure 4.5). A swinging arm or leg, a log bobbing in the water, branches blowing in the wind—even the motion of the moon, sun, and stars—all tend to exhibit arcing motion. Linear movement is unusual in nature and looks artificial when included in a scene.

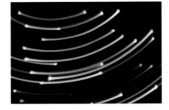

Figure 4.5. Arcs.[1]

I actually take this a step further to say that they all exhibit a type of sinusoidal movement, and that's where the programming comes in. We'll look at ways to implement this in Section 10.2. However, by adding acceleration in the previous example, we have moved from linear velocity to a velocity that arcs over time.

---

[1]Figure 4.5 is provided under Creative Commons License, available at http://stockarch.com/images/abstract/light/streaking-light-arcs-2018.

4.3.4   Follow-Through and Overlapping Action

I like to think of follow-through and overlapping action as the observation of Newton's First Law, which can be paraphrased as, "An object in motion will stay in motion, and an object at rest will stay at rest." This principle helps the artist demonstrate to the viewer that the animated characters are not rigid but instead are made of the same types of materials with which we are familiar.

Imagine the cloak of a rider as he gallops across the scene, the ponytail of a toddler as she runs for a toy, or the gown of a ballroom dancer as she gracefully dances across the hall. The action of the cloak, ponytail, and dress would all look wrong if they moved pixel for pixel with their character. Instead, they should float or bounce a moment behind. The mass of the material combined with the elasticity of the connection to the character result in the actions that flow from the initial action, only slightly delayed and dampened.

While this is something that the artist could add, it might be nearly impossible to anticipate all the player actions. Unlike traditional animation, the secondary action must occur based on some unknown player action. This is where the programmer can come to the rescue. As an example, suppose you are moving a Chinese dragon with a long, flowing tail. The primary action is the player's movement of the dragon's head. The secondary action could be a series of linked tail segments.

Figure 4.6. Dragon's tail as overlapping action

A very simple example of this can be found on the companion website, http://www.2dGraphicsProgramming.com. The image in Figure 4.6 shows that the tail sprites act as secondary actions. The technique to create the tail movement is to simply loop through the tail segment and accelerate toward the current position of the previous segment. Combined with animated sprites that trigger their animation down through the line of segments, you could quickly get a very nice effect.

It might be interesting to note that, taken together, these last three principles of animation are really just the observable phenomena of Newtonian mechanics, applied to art. Applied as a whole and combined with cel animation, you have the possibility of creating a very rich and dynamic scene. For example, combining deceleration into the run animation eventually transitions into an idle animation. In the new animation cycle, the character is stopped but continues to breathe as his chest rises and drops in a steady arch. Finally, add a directional rippling effect to a linked series of sprites that represent his cape blowing in the wind. These cape sprites may lag to his left when he is running to the right, but when he stops they are caught by the wind and move past him to flutter to the right.

While this series of events may only represent a second of game time, the fact that it is an action the player will perform many times throughout the game means that these small details will be significant to the game play experience.

4.4   Animation Cycles

So far we have looked at incorporating only a single animation cycle into a character. In our case, it was a run cycle that works really well for running left and right, but it doesn't look quite right when the character is stopped; the animation will literally stop mid stride.

In a production environment, you have multiple animation cycles per character. Examples of the animation cycles for Newman from the game *aliEnd* are shown in Figure 4.7. This might include cycles for running, attacking, jumping, blocking, and even just standing around. (Often, it is the idle cycle that will endue the most life into your animated character.) You need to create a robust animation system that will allow you to switch between these cycles. In this system, depending on the animation sequences, you may need to end one cycle before continuing on to the next cycle. However, this won't always be the case. For example, if you have just started an animation cycle when the player presses the attack button, waiting until the end of the cycle might result in a system that is not as responsive as the player expects. You will need to work with your artist to design a system that works best for the task at hand.

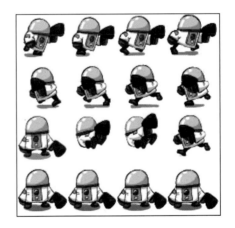

Figure 4.7. *AliEnd*: selection of Newman's various animation cycles.

The good news is that frame-by-frame animation is forgiving. You may have noticed in the examples in this chapter—for example, when the character flips running directions—that it is not as disconcerting as you might otherwise expect it would be. In many cases, the viewer's visual system will unconsciously fill in the gaps, making up for the missing transitions.

Also, keep in mind as you are developing your animation system that you may need multiple sprite sheets to contain your various animation cycles.

4.4.1   Animation in Early Development

During a recent conversation with Brad Graeber, CEO of Powerhourse Animation (a company that specializes in 2D animation for games), I asked the following question: "If you could make one request of the game programmers with whom you often work on projects, what would it be?"

In his reply, Graeber explained that when animators work on films, they often have the opportunity to provide pencil sketches and animated storyboards that are included directly in the early stages of film development, perhaps even before the storyline is completed. Through this, the animators are able to see immediately whether the concept they are working through fits within the context of the film.

Unfortunately, game development never has the technology in place to provide pencil sketches early into the game. The only request by the game development team is for a fully animated finished product. As such, the animators do not have the chance to view and then make changes early in the process because they do not get to see the early animation and pencil sketches in the context of the game.

The request is for us, as game programmers, to ensure that our engines and game systems can support low frame-rate storyboard-style animations during prototyping and early development. In so doing, we could then have an expectation for a better end-product.

I think that is a great suggestion, and hopefully it is something you'll think about as you start to work with artists on your projects. It is a reminder that, in many ways, the discipline of game development is still new, and there is a lot we can still learn from traditional media.

Exercises

Questions

4.1. How many milliseconds pass between cels that are animated to play at 30 fps?

4.1. The sprite sheet for the runner used in the examples in this chapter cannot be programmed to jump over obstacles. Why not?

Challenges

Challenge 4.1. Combine the runner animation with the snowman from the previous examples to create a snow scene. Be sure to implement the principle of slow in/slow out.

Challenge 4.2. Add to the scene created in Challenge 4.1 the ability to throw snowballs. Can you come up with a way to implement gravity on your snowballs to create an arc?

Challenge 4.3. Add a second player to the snowball game. Implement a mode so that the other player, when hit by a snowball, moves in slow motion for 3 seconds. In the slow-motion mode, both the velocity and the animation should move at a slower rate.

Challenge 4.4. Implement a graphics scene that makes use of follow-through and overlapping action.

Challenge 4.5. We have seen that many of the principles of animation can be thought of as the observational results of Newton's Laws of Motion. However, none of them mentions Newton's Third Law (paraphrased as, "For every action there is an equal and opposite reaction." Your challenge is to implement a game scene that makes use of the third law. *Hint:* What happens when a character fires a missile from a tank? What should happen to a floating platform if a player jumps from one platform to the next?

Challenge 4.6. Investigate various pixel deltas and animation speeds. Are your results similar to what is shown in Figure 4.3?

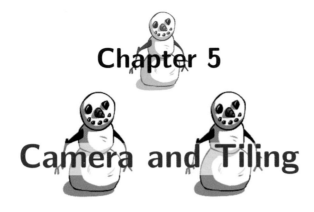

Chapter 5

Camera and Tiling

5.1   A Simple Camera

This chapter shows how easy it can be to create a simple game camera, although a camera isn't needed unless the game world is bigger than the screen. This first example once again uses our runner and snowman assets to create a very simple scene that is wide enough to require a game camera. To keep the example simple, let's start with our original animation sequence and the example in Section 4.2.

We will add code to the example. Make sure you have both the run_cycle and snow_assets sprite sheets added to your content folder and then add the following member variables:

```
//..

//Source Data
private Texture2D  runCycleTexture;
private Rectangle  currentCelLocation;
private Vector2    runnerCelOrigin;

private Texture2D  snowmanTexture;
private Rectangle  snowmanCelLocation;
private Vector2    snowmanCelOrigin;

//Destination Data
private Vector2 runnerPosition;
private Vector2[] snowmenPositions = new Vector2[10];

//Camera Data
private Vector2 cameraPosition;
private Vector2 cameraOffset;

//Animation Data
//...
```

Figure 5.1. Camera offset.

The above code snippet has the old `runCycleTexture` and also has a new snowman texture and associated source data. This time we also add ten snowmen with their positions stored in an array of `Vector2`s.

You may also notice an extra `Vector2` in the code to store the origin source data for the runner. That will ensure that the runner ends up truly in the center of the screen instead of offset down and to the right, as in Figure 5.1.

The last set of variables are for tracking the camera. The camera has a position within the game world, and our scene will be focused on the camera's position. So in order to center the screen on the camera, we also need to know the location of the center of the screen. This is the value we store in the camera offset: the center of the screen, with position (screen width/2, screen height/2).

With all the various numbers we are tracking, it may take a moment to think about which values are represented and where they originate. Figure 5.1 may help to bring it all into focus.

The black line, with a value of (128, 128) on it, notes the sprite source data (the x-value is actually going to be a multiple of 128 as we move through the animation cycle on the sprite sheet. The green line represents `runnerPosition` as measured from the game origin. Notice that the origin (0, 0) is no longer located in the top-left corner. This is because we are using the new camera offset value (represented by the red value). We will look at how this is implemented in our Draw calls in a moment. The runner position and camera position are both located at (0, 128).

The area of the image that is grayed out is there only to illustrate the section of the screen that would previously have been unseen. It won't actually show up grayed out in your scene.

In order to get this all to work, we need a few more steps, but first we must initialize the values:

```
currentCelLocation = new Rectangle(0, 0, 128, 128);
runnerCelOrigin = new Vector2(64, 64);

snowmanCelLocation = new Rectangle(0, 128, 256, 256);
snowmanCelOrigin = new Vector2(128, 128);

runnerPosition = new Vector2(100, 100);
cameraOffset = new Vector2(400, 240); //half the screen size
cameraPosition = runnerPosition;

for (int i = 0; i < 10; i++)
    snowmenPositions[i] = new Vector2(200 * i, 200);
```

We also have spaced the ten snowmen evenly along the x-axis, 200 pixels apart.

You might have noticed that we did not initialize `cameraPosition` in this code snippet. Since we want to focus on the player, we set the camera's position to be the same as the player's position. This is the only change we need to make to the Update function.

```
//..

cameraPosition = runnerPosition;

base.Update(gameTime);
}
```

Now we need to add the snowmen Draw calls in our Draw code. The loop is included below, but you should notice one more modification: the location where we are drawing the runner is no longer simply `runnerPosition`. We are now subtracting the camera position from the runner's position.

```
Vector2 drawLocation = cameraPosition - cameraOffset;
spriteBatch.Begin();
spriteBatch.Draw(runCycleTexture,
  runnerPosition - drawLocation,
  currentCelLocation,
  Color.White,
  0.0f,                //Rotation
  snowmanCelOrigin,
  1.0f,                //scale
  eRunnerSprEff,
  1.0f);
for (int i = 0; i < 10; i++)
{
    spriteBatch.Draw(snowmanTexture,
      snowmenPositions[i] - drawLocation,
      snowmanCelLocation,
      Color.White,
```

```
       0.0f,                        //Rotation
       snowmanCelOrigin,
20     1.0f,                        //scale
       SpriteEffects.None,
       1.0f);
}
spriteBatch.End();
```

As a last step, make sure you're loading both textures in the content load:

```
1   runCycleTexture = Content.Load<Texture2D>("run_cycle");
    snowmanTexture = Content.Load<Texture2D>("snow_assets");
```

Now we have a camera that travels with the runner, and the rest of the game world seems to move around him.

A discerning reader may notice a mathematical curiosity in the previous code samples. In the Update function, we set the camera position as follows:

$$cameraPosition = runnerPosition .$$

But later, in the Draw call, we create a draw location

$$drawLocation = cameraPosition - cameraOffset$$

and then finally draw at the location as defined by

$$final\ draw\ location = runnerPosition - cameraPosition.$$

The result would seem to be

$$draw\ location = runnerPosition - (runnerPosition - cameraOffset),$$

and sure enough, we can see that the end result is that the player is drawn at the location of the camera offset. So if the values cancel each other out, why not just use

$$draw\ location = cameraOffset?$$

If it appears that the values we set for the runner position and camera position are completely ignored, well, yes, they are to an extent. Setting the camera position to be equal to the runner's position is the culprit. Let's now look at some examples of when we might want a different camera location.

Perhaps we want to indicate to the players that they have reached the end of the level. In that case, we may want to clamp the camera value to a certain range. Then we should add something such as the following into our update:

```
if (cameraPosition.X > 1000)
    cameraPosition.X = 1000;
if (cameraPosition.X < 0)
    cameraPosition.X = 0;
```

By preventing the camera from moving beyond a given range, we are able to give players a cue as to where they should and should not be headed.

5.1.1   Smoother Camera Movement

Another issue might be a game that has fast action. Locking a camera to a character that quickly darts back and forth can be a bit annoying. Try it out for yourself by changing the velocity modifiers from 2 to 20 and then try running back and forth.

```
if (Keyboard.GetState().IsKeyDown(Keys.Left))
{
    bIsRunning = true;
    runnerPosition.X -= 20; ;
    eRunnerSprEff = SpriteEffects.FlipHorizontally;
}
else if (Keyboard.GetState().IsKeyDown(Keys.Right))
{
    bIsRunning = true;
    runnerPosition.X += 20;
    eRunnerSprEff = SpriteEffects.None;
}
```

As you can see, that's not a very pleasant experience for the player. One possible solution is to replace the line with code that will cause the camera to move at a speed relative to the distance it is from the player. In my testing, I found 0.05 was a good constant to use for the multiplier.

```
//Vector2 goalCameraPosition = runnerPosition - cameraOffset;

const float MULTIPLIER = 0.05f;

if (cameraPosition.X < runnerPosition.X)
{
    cameraPosition.X -=
    ((cameraPosition.X - runnerPosition.X) * MULTIPLIER);
}
else if (cameraPosition.X > runnerPosition.X)
{
    cameraPosition.X
    += ((cameraPosition.X - runnerPosition.X) * -MULTIPLIER);
}
```

Note that this code restricts the camera movement to the x-axis. If you want vertical camera movement, you will need to add that here as well.

5.1.2   Jumping and Ground Tracking

There are two schools of thought about what to do in a platformer when a game character jumps beyond the top of the screen. Here are the obvious options; you may be able to think of others:

Figure 5.2. Y-axis camera tracking: option 1 (left) and option 2 (right).

1. Track the player in the y-axis (Figure 5.2, left): An easy solution is to just have the camera track the player into the vertical space. In this case, it is likely that the game view will no longer include the ground for a very high jump. It will have gone off screen as you track the jumper.

2. Don't track the player in the y-axis (Figure 5.2, right): In this case, you will lose track of the player into the clouds. We are used to having the player in the scene, so this would be an odd choice.

Your choice depends on your game play, but the experts report that option 2 actually feels much more natural than you might expect [Rasmussen 05]. Players don't like to lose sight of the ground. When you start to fall, you want to know where the obstacles are and you want to have time to avoid them. If the camera is tracking the player, the ground and associated dangers are obscured until it's too late for the player to react. You should be able to find examples of games that do both.

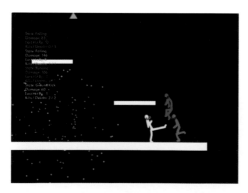

Figure 5.3. Player tracking by Gunther Fox.

Perhaps the best solution is to zoom the camera out so that you can track both the player and the ground. Of course, assuming you have built zoom functionality into your 2D graphics engine (we haven't yet), this would be the best solution. However, you might not want to resize your game scene in this way.

In his four-player game *Super Stash Bros* [Fox 10], Gunther Fox employs a combination of two techniques for tracking players, which are shown in Figure 5.3. First, a dynamic camera zooms in and out based on the distance between the players. There is a maximum zoom distance, beyond which the players may be off the screen. If this occurs, an arrow indicates the player's location.

5.2   Simple Camera Zoom

When we discuss pixel shaders in Section 9.5.4, we will look at a more robust technique for zooming the camera. In the meantime, a simple option is to make use of the ability to scale the entire sprite batch.

But before we do, it's important to take a moment to consider the ramifications of dynamic scaling. That is, there is no longer a 1:1 ratio between the texels in the texture and the pixels on the screen. This may not be significant, depending on art style, but it is something to consider. As we noted in Chapter 3, there are issues with scaling up and scaling down.

Continuing with the camera code we developed earlier in this chapter, we add camera-zoom functionality by making use of a scaling matrix. A *matrix* is a mathematical construct that comes from the field of linear algebra. Matrices are essential to 3D graphics and are beyond the scope of this book. All we need to know at this point is that a matrix stores a set of numbers in a way that they can contain information about how to move, scale, or rotate a point in 2D or 3D space.

Before we create the matrix, however, we need to track the zoom amount. To do this, we add the following to our code in the appropriate locations:

```
//Add member function
private float fZoomLevel;

//...

//Add to Initialize()
fZoomLevel = 1.0f;

//...

//Add to Update()
if (Keyboard.GetState().IsKeyDown(Keys.Up))
{
    fZoomLevel += 0.01f;
}
else if (Keyboard.GetState().IsKeyDown(Keys.Down))
{
    fZoomLevel -= 0.01f;
}

//...

//Replace drawLocation calculation in Draw()
Vector2 drawLocation = cameraPosition - (cameraOffset/
    fZoomLevel);
```

Now we need to create a matrix and use it in the `spriteBatch.Begin()` call. Unfortunately, the overloaded Begin function that includes a matrix parameter needs a variety of other parameters as well, making it look more scary than it is. If we just add the following parameters, we should see some good results (the mathematical scaling magic happens in the last parameter).

```
spriteBatch.Begin(SpriteSortMode.Deferred,
                  BlendState.NonPremultiplied,
                  SamplerState.PointClamp,
                  DepthStencilState.Default,
                  RasterizerState.CullNone,
                  null,
                  Matrix.CreateScale(fZoomLevel));
```

This is actually a great place to test out the various sampler states described in Section 3.4.1. Try modifying the sampler state in the above code to see the results.

5.3   Tiling

By making use of a game camera moving along the x-axis, we have experimented with a graphical design that is familiar in side-scrollers. This could easily be converted into a y-axis camera such as the one used in such games as *Mega Jump* [Get Set Games Inc. 11].

5.3.1   Simple 2D Tiled Graphics

By utilizing another genre familiar to older gamers, we can now implement the tile graphics of the early *Ultima* games [Garriott 81] and *Legend of Zelda* [Miyamoto and Tezuka 86]. This type of top-down tile graphics is also used in more modern games, such as *Civilization Revolution* [Firaxis 09].

In these games, the camera is directly overhead and the tiles are often more symbolic than realistic, similar to viewing a traditional map. This type of perspective may be referred to as "god view" (see Figure 5.4) If the system includes a graphical *fog of war*, the perspective may be referred to as a "strategic view." A third option, used in some of the early games, is to incorporate the line of sight from the perspective of the player, so that the hidden objects are not revealed see Figure 5.5.

To generate a simple god-view perspective with tiled graphics, we need

1. a set of tile sprites for the various types of terrain,

2. a map of how those tiles should be distributed,

3. a draw routine that draws only the tiles that are in the field of view.

Figure 5.4. Search: tile graphics.

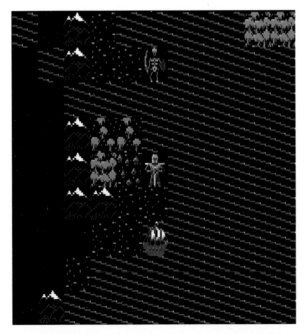

Figure 5.5. Search: tile graphics with line of sight.

At this point I assume that you can include the sprite loading and initialization yourself and further that you can work through a way to store sprites in a class. Look at the following class definition and fill in the blanks as appropriate. We will use this class in our example.

```
 1   class cSpriteClass
     {
          private Texture2D mTexture;
          private Rectangle mLocation;
 5        private Vector2 mOrigin;
          public Color mColor;

          public cSpriteClass() {\\..\\}

10        public void LoadContent(ContentManager pContent, String
              fileName, Rectangle pLocation, Vector2 pOrigin)
              {\\..\\}

          public void Draw(SpriteBatch pBatch, Vector2
              pGameLocation, float pRotation, float pScale)
              {\\..\\}
     }
```

In this example we create a god-view tank game, similar to Figure 5.6, by utilizing four sprites for terrain (plains, hills, mountains, and water) and one for the tank.

As before, we use a camera system that includes a position that follows the player and a zoom feature. In addition, we need to distinguish be-

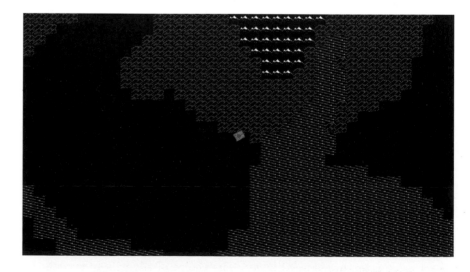

Figure 5.6. Two-dimensional tile graphics tank game.

tween the player's position on the map and the player's position in screen coordinates.

For this example I list only code that is significantly different than anything we've covered in the past. You will need to fill in the gaps on your own.

At a minimum, you need to add the following member variables in order to draw the sprites:

```
1  //Source Data
   cSpriteClass plains, mountains, hills, water, player;

   //Destination Data
5  private Vector2 playerMapPosition, playerScreenPosition;
   private float playerForwardVelocity;
```

I have also added the following values for moving the tank:

```
1  private float playerForwardVelocity;
   private float playerRotation;
   private float maxPlayerVelocity;
```

In addition, it is helpful to put the width and height values that remain constant in one place. If we ever need to change them, it will be much easier having them grouped together. It also helps to prevent the use of magic numbers.

```
1   //Size of the game window
    private const int SCREEN_W = 1280;
    private const int SCREEN_H = 720;

5   //Size of an individual sprite tile
    private const int SPRITE_W = 32;
    private const int SPRITE_H = 32;

    //Size of the game map
10  private const int MAP_W = 256;
    private const int MAP_H = 256;
```

This last bit is used for loading and storing the game map.

```
1  //Game Map
   Texture2D mapTexture;
   private Color[] gameMap = new Color[MAP_W * MAP_H];
```

There are many ways to store a game map; in this case I have chosen to make use of a 2D texture (Figure 5.7). This is a convenient format because, like a map, a texture is a 2D array. The choice of tile will be encoded as color information.

Figure 5.7. Example texture image used as game map, map01.png: R = 255 for mountains, R = 128 for hills, G = 255 for forest, and B = 255 for water.

A discerning computer scientist may note that this choice requires significantly more space in computer memory than should be necessary. Even if we had 256 different terrain types, we should need an array comprised only of byte-sized elements, not 4-byte RGBA. This is true, but as a result of our memory-intensive choice, we gain a few advantages:

1. We can use any raster-based graphics editor to create and edit the game map.

2. We already have built-in functionality for working with Texture2D type.

3. We gain experience storing nongraphical data in a texture.

Each platform and game requirement is different, however. It is also unlikely that a raster-based graphics editor will be a sufficient tool for complex maps. It is your responsibility, as the graphics programmer, to understand the needs of the system, the expectations of your team, and your own resource limitations. Taking these all into account, you can then choose and build the most appropriate system.

Continuing with our example, in the game constructor, you need to set up the game window and create the new sprite class objects. For example:

```
graphics = new GraphicsDeviceManager(this);

//Set game window size
graphics.PreferredBackBufferWidth = SCREEN_W;
graphics.PreferredBackBufferHeight = SCREEN_H;

plains = new cSpriteClass();
//Repeat above for each terrain type
```

In the LoadContent function, you need to load the sprite data and map. The following code provides an example of the plains tile. You will need to repeat it for the other terrain types and the player tank, and you will need to modify the rectangle as appropriate based on the sprite's location on the sprite sheet.

```
plains.LoadContent(Content,
                   "tiledSprites",
                   new Rectangle(0, 0, SPRITE_W, SPRITE_H),
                   new Vector2(SPRITE_W / 2, SPRITE_H / 2));
//Repeat above for each terrain type and the player

mapTexture = Content.Load<Texture2D>("map01");
mapTexture.GetData<Color>(gameMap);
```

The last line in the above code snippet will copy the data in the texture directly into the large array of colors we defined earlier. This will be used as your game map.

In the game update, include player input controls to change the player's rotation and velocity. Once you have the new rotation and velocity, it's easy to move the player in map coordinates by using the sine and cosine trigonometry functions:

$$\Delta x\text{-position} = \text{forward velocity} \times \cos(\text{rotation}) \times \text{elapsed seconds},$$

$$\Delta y\text{-position} = \text{forward velocity} \times \sin(\text{rotation}) \times \text{elapsed seconds}.$$

By multiplying each value by the elapsed seconds, we can ensure that the velocity remains the same regardless of frame rate. In code, this looks like

```
//Update Player Rotation from Keyboard Input
if (Keyboard.GetState().IsKeyDown(Keys.Left))
{
    playerRotation -= (playerRotationRate
                        * gameTime.ElapsedGameTime.TotalSeconds
                        );
}
else if (Keyboard.GetState().IsKeyDown(Keys.Right))
{
    playerRotation += (playerRotationRate
                        * gameTime.ElapsedGameTime.TotalSeconds
                        );
}

//Update Player Velocity from Keyboard Input
if (Keyboard.GetState().IsKeyDown(Keys.Up))
{
    if (playerForwardVelocity <= maxPlayerVelocity)
        playerForwardVelocity += 0.5f;

}

//Update Player Position on Map
playerMapPosition.X += (float)(playerForwardVelocity
                        * Math.Cos(playerRotation)
                        * gameTime.ElapsedGameTime.
                        TotalSeconds);
playerMapPosition.Y += (float)(playerForwardVelocity
                        * Math.Sin(playerRotation)
                        * gameTime.ElapsedGameTime.
                        TotalSeconds);
```

By keeping the player's position in relation to the map, we will later be able to compare the player's position with the terrain at that location. But for now, we need to convert those coordinates into screen coordinates in order to draw the player at the correct position. We also update the camera position as before.

```
1   //Convert from map to screen coordinates
    playerScreenPosition.X = playerMapPosition.X * SPRITE_W;
    playerScreenPosition.Y = playerMapPosition.Y * SPRITE_H;

5   cameraPosition = playerScreenPosition;
```

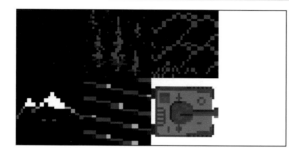

Figure 5.8. Sprites used in this example. Note the required white space on the right. This was done to ensure the texture remained a power of two (128×64).

Finally, we need to draw the sprites for the tiles and player (Figure 5.8). This involves looping through the map and drawing the appropriate sprite in the appropriate location. However, we don't want to draw the entire map—only the area that is visible around the player. For our example, that includes about 23 sprites on the left and right of the player and 15 above and below the player.

In that case, we need to modify the normal i and j for loop with the appropriate values:

```
1   Vector2 screenLocation;
    Color mapLocation;

    int xOffset = 23;
5   int yOffset = 13;

    int iStart = (int)(playerMapPosition.X - xOffset);
    if (iStart < 0) iStart = 0;

10  int iEnd = (int)(playerMapPosition.X + xOffset);
    if (iEnd >= MAP_W) iEnd = MAP_W - 1;

    int jStart = (int)(playerMapPosition.Y - yOffset);
    if (jStart < 0) jStart = 0;
15
    int jEnd = (int)(playerMapPosition.Y + yOffset);
    if (jEnd >= MAP_H) jEnd = MAP_H - 1;

    for (int i = iStart; i < iEnd; i++)
20    for (int j = jStart; j < jEnd; j++)
      {
        //Draw appropriate tile for this location
      }

25  //Draw player on top of tiled surface
    player.Draw(spriteBatch, playerScreenPosition - drawLocation,
        (float)playerRotation, 1.0f);
```

Now for the details of the Draw call. Let's consider only the mountains and plains for now and assume that we have a map (stored in a texture) such that red pixels indicate mountains. If the pixel is not a mountain, it must be a plain. In that case, our Draw call in the middle of the above loop would look something like this:

```
screenLocation = new Vector2(i * SPRITE_W, j * SPRITE_H);

mapLocation = gameMap[i + (j * MAP_H)];

if (mapColor.R == 255)
    mountains.Draw(spriteBatch, screenLocation - drawLocation
        );
else
    plains.Draw(spriteBatch, screenLocation - drawLocation);
```

You can add the logic for the other color and tiles yourself. You could even go so far as to combine the color combinations. For example, a red value of 128 might indicate hills and a green value of 255 might indicate vegetation. The vegetation sprite could then be layered on top of the hill sprite.

5.3.2 Overlapping Tiles

Occasionally, some game developers have chosen to implement an overlapping tile-based graphics. Game designer Daniel Cook offers a set of these on his website[1] as well as some instructions on how they map together. The result is some amazing-looking environments, as can be seen in Figure 5.9.

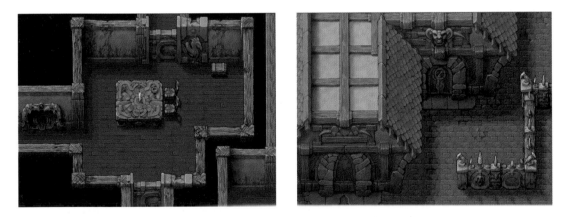

Figure 5.9. Art from *2D Circle Graphic Archive* by Daniel Cook (Lostgarden.com).

---

[1]http://www.lostgarden.com/2006/07/more-free-game-graphics.html

5.3.3 Hexagonal Tiles

Instead of allowing for the type of continuous movement demonstrated in the example above, a feature of many tile games is that they allow for turn-based game play, in which units are on either one tile or another tile, but never between tiles. For example, in this type of game, the player's unit may be allowed to move across n number of tiles on each turn. Unfortunately, square grid–based movement has some limitations. One of the major issues is that units that are across grid corners from one another are not equidistant to those that are on side-by-side lines, resulting in extra rules and unnatural game play. So instead, many tabletop games make use of a hexagonal grid, which allows for six equidistant faces for every game tile.

Consequently, hexagonal grids are seen in many turn-based war games, where they provide a more strategically compelling experience. An example is the open source game *Battle for Wesnoth* [White 05] (Figure 5.10).

While slightly more challenging to code, a hexagonal grid works in a similar fashion as the square grid equivalent except that it can't easily be mapped to 2D array and therefore requires the creation of additional level editing tools.

Figure 5.10. Screenshot of the video game *Battle for Wesnoth* (version 1.8.1).[2]

5.3.4 Line of Sight

Another feature of early games was the blocked line of sight that would occur as you moved through the world. This works well if you want to hide objects from the player but maintain the top-down perspective (as seen in Figure 5.5).

Personally, I really like the end result of this technique, but perhaps that's because I'm an old-school gamer. I think it helps to create a connection between the players and their avatars in the game world. It's a technique I haven't seen used much in modern games, though.

There are different options to implement this technique, and some are more efficient than others. The goal is to decide before drawing a particular sprite whether it should be hidden from view. In other words, does that tile have a line of sight to the player? Without giving away too much of a solution, see whether you can design your own system. This problem is included as a challenge at the end of this chapter.

---

[2] *Wesnoth* screenshot published under GNU General Public License. Source: http:// wesnoth.org.

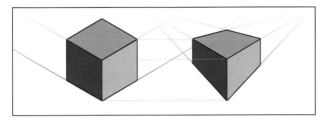

Figure 5.11. Projection comparison: isometric projection featuring parallel vanishing points (left) and two-point perspective featuring foreshortening (right).

5.4 Isometric Tiled Graphics

Isometric projection is a method for representing a 3D object in 2D space (see Figure 5.11, left). We discuss much more about perspective and depth in Chapter 6, but let's take a look here at the isometric format as it is often used in tiled games. The most famous example from recent years is *FarmVille* [Zynga 09].

Isometric projection is a type of parallel projection, meaning that the perspective assumes a camera at an infinite distance. The result is that there is no foreshortening (all objects appear the same size no matter how far away they are; see Figure 5.11, right). The term *isometric* (of equal measures) refers to the fact that in these drawings, the width, height, and depth are all drawn at the same scale. As a result, an isometric perspective is often used in engineering drawings when a 3D perspective is needed but accurate line scale must be maintained regardless of distance.

Another famous, albeit significantly older game example that makes use of an isometric perspective is the arcade game *Q*bert* [Davis and Lee 82].

The projection angles may be adjusted, but typical isometric projection is created by producing grid lines at 30 and 60 degrees for a total of 120 degrees between the front faces of the tile. This can be used to create a tiled game map. As you can see in Figure 5.12, an advantage of the isometric tile

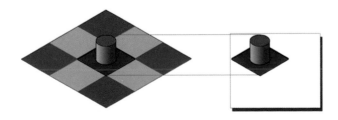

Figure 5.12. Isometric tile with height mapped onto a sprite sheet.

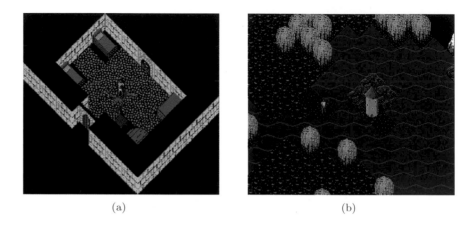

(a)   (b)

Figure 5.13. A 45 degree isometric tiled graphics game prototype: (a) inside and (b) outside.

is that it may have a height component. When drawn in the appropriate order (back to front), the front tiles may overlap the back tiles.

Figure 5.13 shows screenshots from a prototype I worked on that used 45-degree grid lines instead of the standard 30/60. They also provide good examples of overlapping and how well line of sight can work when the player is in the interior of a building. Here, I limited the height of most game objects to the conceptual cubic area that can be seen in the wall segments. The only exception to this is the tower in Figure 5.13(b).

There is really no limit to the height of the tiles in an isometric game, however. Large towers can be mixed with flat tiles, each taking up varying amounts of space on the sprite sheet. The only significant concern is related to game play, ensuring that the front tiles do not cover up anything important to game play.

The game *CastleVille* [Zynga Dallas 11] regularly has very high towers and other obstacles that obscure the view of the tiles behind it. This issue has been addressed, though, by creating an outline feature that supports any important object that is otherwise obscured.

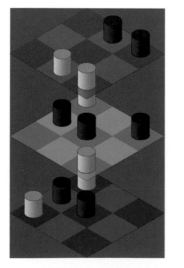

Figure 5.14. Layered isometric game concept.

You could take it even further with multiple layers and the use of the alpha channel. Figure 5.14 is a mockup of such a game. It would be interesting to see what kind of dungeon or tower game could be made by implementing something like this.

5.4.1 Limits of Isometric Perspective

The feature of isometric perspective that it does not have foreshortened sides is useful when creating a tiled game, but it has some limitations in depth perception. The result is an ambiguity that has been famously exploited to create an apparent paradox, which can be seen in M. C. Escher's painting *Ascending and Descending* (lithograph, 1960) and then again later in his *The Waterfall* (lithograph, 1961).

These so-called impossible images were inspired by the combined work of Roger Penrose and his father Lionel Penrose. Roger, after having attended a conference that included presentations by the not-yet-famous Escher, went home to create the Penrose triangle. He showed it to his father, who then created the Penrose stairs, a never-ending staircase. The images were eventually published in the *British Journal of Psychology*. Roger sent the article to Escher, who then incorporated the impossible staircase concept into his aforementioned works [Seckel 07], the seed of this idea creating its own cyclical triangle.

With this in mind, I think it would be very interesting to create an isometric tile–based game that made use of this type of warped perspective. Although it might be difficult to wrap your head around such a game, both as a developer and as a player, it seems entirely possible and may create some interesting game-play mechanics.

Exercises: Challenges

Challenge 5.1. Add a jumping feature to the camera example in Section 5.1. Implement the two options for y-axis camera movement (track the player and don't track the player), allowing the user to toggle the y-axis camera movement during runtime. Add an arrow to track players when they are off-screen.

Challenge 5.2. Complete the tiled program example in Section 5.3, implementing zoom controls and adding your own set of tiled graphical sprites to represent other terrain types. As discussed at the very end of that section, implement layered sprites so that vegetation can be mapped over terrain.

Challenge 5.3. Add line of sight to the tiled program example in Section 5.3 such that mountains completely block the line of sight.

Challenge 5.4. Expand the line-of-sight program from Challenge 5.3 so that in addition, after passing through three in a row, hills and trees will also block the view. Add an exception to this rule so that when the player is standing on a hill, it takes six in a row to block the player's line of sight.

Challenge 5.5. Implement an isometric tiled graphics program.

Challenge 5.6. Implement an isometric game that makes use of the limitations of the isometric perspective to generate impossible structures. At a minimum, add enough functionality so that the player can navigate through your impossible world.

Chapter 6

The Illusion of Depth

So far, we have covered the basic systems required for building a simple 2D graphics engine capable of rendering and animating sprites. We're able to maintain and track multiple sprites, sourced from larger sprite sheets, and our sprites animate smoothly, even across different frame rates.

However, the engine is still limited. Even high-quality artwork produces a rendered scene that looks flat. For the vast majority of games in the 1980s, this was the status quo. Incremental graphical improvements were achieved by higher resolution or an increased color palette. Examples include Richard Garriott's *Ultima IV*, Alexey Pajitnov's *Tetris*, and Shigeru Miyamoto and Takashi Tezuka's *Legend of Zelda*. But as a fledgling industry, these small teams of game developers didn't yet make use of the long-established illusionary techniques developed in art or film.

We have already taken a peek at some possible depth creation through the implementation of overlapping tiled graphics and isometric perspective. In this chapter, we take a step back in time and focus on the numerous techniques we can borrow from the more traditional graphical disciplines in order to apply the illusion of depth into a variety of game genres.

6.1 A Historical Perspective on Perspective

Evolution has trained our brains to create meaningful patterns out of the millions of photons that land on our retinas. This may have been an issue of survival for early man, but for the last thousand years, humans have studied and eventually began to master the techniques that cause us to perceive depth on a flat canvas.

In 1021, mathematician Ibn al-Haytham (Alhazen) wrote the *Book of Optics*, a text based on experimentation and observation that—for the first time—described how light enters the eye and may be transmitted and

Figure 6.1. *A View of the Progress of the Water Castle Julia*, Giovanni Battista Piranesi (eighteenth century).

perceived by the brain. This book paved the way for the science of visual perception, a field crossing both psychology and biology with the goal of understanding how our visual system works and how that information is processed by the brain.

In the fifteenth century, Leonardo Da Vinci continued this work, adding an understanding of peripheral vision. The nineteenth-century physiologist and physicist Hermann von Helmholtz is given credit for being the first to note that our brain unconsciously constructs a three-dimensional representation of our surroundings from the surprisingly limited amount of information received by the optic system. He explained that the mind achieves this perception of depth through a series of visual assumptions. For example, when we watch a squirrel disappear behind a tree, we unconsciously understand that the tree must exist in a physical space between us and the squirrel because of our assumption that closer objects will block the view of more distant objects.

Early artists used the mathematics of perspective to create both beautiful landscapes and detailed cityscapes. (See Figures 6.1 and 6.2 for two examples.)

Thus, although our game engine is restricted to two dimensions, many techniques can assist us in creating our own illusion of depth.

Figure 6.2. *Christ Handing the Keys to St. Peter*, Pietro Perugino, (1481–1482).

6.2 Layering

Perhaps the simplest way to create depth is to add a background image "behind the action."

To keep things simple, let's start once again with just the animation example from Section 4.2, and add the snow_bg.png image to the content folder. Add a Texture2D to track it, load the texture in the LoadContent function, then add the appropriate Draw call. only the Draw call is listed in the code below.

```
//Add member variable:
private Texture2D snowBGTexture;

//...

//Add to LoadContent:
snowBGTexture = Content.Load<Texture2D>("snow_bg");

//Add to Draw:
spriteBatch.Draw(snowBGTexture, Vector2.Zero, Color.White);

//...
```

You may notice that the provided background image includes a few perspective techniques. We go into those in more detail later in this chapter.

But first, see whether you can incorporate a camera into this image. You need to horizontally tile the background as well as incorporate the camera's position into the draw position for the background. The result should be a fairly simple effect of the player appearing to walk across the landscape.

Figure 6.3. Layering: game-play elements plus background only.

Now add a few game-play elements at the same level as the player. The results should be similar to Figure 6.3, in that there becomes a clear distinction between what's happening at the game-play level and the graphics that makes up the background.

A perfect example of how a simple background can add depth to a game can be seen in the original *Super Mario Bros* [Miyamoto and Tezuka 85]. Interestingly, in the background in that game, the shape of the cloud is repeated in the shape of the bushes.

6.2.1 Foreground

Another common technique is to add a third layer on top of the game-play layer to display information relevant to the player. This layer becomes the GUI for the game, and a variety of styles can be implemented. The foreground choice can have a surprisingly significant effect on the gamer's experience. We explore options for the GUI in much more detail in Chapter 7.

It is not a requirement that the foreground also be a GUI, however. Consider instead a foreground that simply provides a layer on top of the game-play layer. In Figure 6.4, for example, by adding a pair of out-of-focus snowmen as a foreground layer, the result is that the game layer is pushed back into the scene, once again creating a layer of depth. As a final comparison, Figure 6.5 a screenshot of the same image with a foreground only.

Figure 6.4. Layering: game play plus background and foreground.

Figure 6.5. Layering: game play elements plus foreground only.

In these very simplistic examples, the background and foreground layers are static. As you build your engine, you may want to provide the option for the layers to be animated as well.

6.3   The Six Principles of Depth

The previous section looked at depth created outside of the game-play environment. This section examines what I call the *six principles of depth* for 2D games, along with simple techniques for implementing each of the principles within the game-play layer. These six principles are

1. overlap,

2. base height (vertical perspective),

3. scale,

4. atmosphere,

5. focus,

6. parallax.

These six principles are a simplified subset of what are called *monocular cues*, the visual triggers that provide depth information when viewing a scene with one eye. We look briefly at the study of perspective, including a few rules that govern how these principles may be combined to create realistic scenes.

6.3.1   Overlap

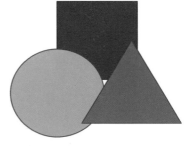

Overlap is a simple concept—so simple that it's easy to overlook its importance. Figure 6.6 shows three shapes, and it is immediately apparent that the blue triangle is in front of the green circle, which is in turn in front of the red square. Without the use of relative sizes, shadowing, or tricks of perspective, we are nevertheless absolutely clear on which shape is in front and which shape is in back simply due to overlapping.

We have already seen that we can control the overlapping of sprites in one of two ways. The easiest is to use the draw order, knowing that where the final rendered screen pixels are the same, the pixel color defined by the red square will be overwritten when the pixel color is redefined by the blue triangle.

Figure 6.6. Depth principle 1: overlap.

The second option is to make use of the sprite depth in the Draw call. On the graphics card, this is done by maintaining a separate 2D array of floats with values from 0.0 to 1.0. This 2D array (called the *depth buffer*) is generated automatically and available for the graphics programmer's use. Every time a pixel is drawn to the screen, a corresponding depth value is entered into the depth buffer. When the depth check is activated, the next time a sprite needs to draw a color in that same pixel, the current sprite's depth is compared against the depth already stored in the depth buffer. Based on that comparison, a decision is made as to whether ignore, replace, or blend the new color.

In XNA, we have seen that the sprite batch allows us to sort the sprites (`BackToFront`, `FrontToBack`, or `Texture`) as well as a blend mode. In OpenGL and DirectX we would be more likely to simply use the depth buffer directly. In any case, the concept is the same and is important for tracking and rendering sprites with the appropriate overlap.

Other scientific terms for the principle of overlap are *occlusion* and *interposition*.

6.3.2   Base Height

Figure 6.7. Depth principle 2: base height.

The next significant principle in determining the distance of a sprite on the screen uses vertical perspective or the sprite's *base height*. Consider the images in Figure 6.7, which shows three snowmen of equal size. It appears that of the three, one of them is farther back than the others, even though no overlap is occurring.

When you think of the definition of perspective, you might be tempted to define it as an optical illusion by which objects that are farther from the camera appear to be smaller than those that are closer to the camera. Yet, in Figure 6.7, a fourth snowman is included at a smaller scale but we are not tempted to think of it as being farther away. On the contrary, it appears to be closer to the camera than the other three.

This is because our mind assumes that the four snowmen all are resting on the same surface. Without any other visual cues, that is a natural assumption and fits our unconscious understanding of the world. Put simply, the lower the base of an object in our field of view, the closer it must be.

Final Fight [Capcom 89] and similar side-scrolling beat-'em-ups use only a combination of overlap and base height to display the depth of each character. This is significant because the player's distance from the camera is an integral aspect of the game play: two game characters must be at the same depth for the attacks to make contact. A more recent example is *Castle Crashers* [The Behemoth 08], in which the characters can move within a range of depth. The best example of base height is in *Plants vs. Zombies* [PopCap Games 09], in which the perspective of depth is very clear, despite the fact that the entire play area is built only on base height and overlap. In all of these cases, distant players are no smaller in scale than their closer counterparts, yet the depth of play is clear.

After overlap, the principle of base height is also one of the earliest techniques used to demonstrate depth in early paintings. It is in this context that the technique is more often called *vertical perspective*. Vertical perspective is often associated with the art of ancient Egypt, in which scale was reserved for signifying the importance of the person represented in the image. Nearer figures are shown at a lower base height than larger, more distant figures. For example, in Figure 6.8, the images of Senejem and his wife are painted at a very large scale, but they are overlapped by the smaller figures drawn with a lower base height.

Figure 6.8. Depth principle 2: base height used in ancient Egyptian art from the Tomb of Senejem.

The exception to the base height principle can be seen in Figure 6.9, in which the apparent closeness of the smaller object is no longer a certainty. Two significant features of this figure cause the smaller balloon to now appear to be a more distant object. First, because the content is hot air balloons, our brain knows it is possible that we are perceiving the images as in the air. When an object is no longer secured to a surface, the base height rule does not hold true. This assumption is reinforced by the lack of shadows under the object.

A second feature that changes the illusion of depth in Figure 6.9 is that our experience tells us that any two hot air balloons are normally about the same size. Unless we are in a fantasy environment that has miniature baskets for miniature people, we know that the smaller object must be farther away due to its relative size when compared to the apparently larger ones. This was not a problem for the snowmen example in which our experience tells us that smaller-sized snowmen are possible.

Figure 6.9. Depth principle 2: base height exception.

Figure 6.10. Depth principle 2: base height exception with overlap.

However, even the exceptional features present in Figure 6.9 can be outweighed by the first principle of overlap, as can be seen in Figure 6.10. Despite our knowledge that hot air balloons should all be about the same size, the overlap shows that in this particular environment, they can be different sizes.

Note that the lack of overlap is not the only distinction between Figures 6.7 and 6.9. Importantly, there were no evident shadows in the latter. Shadows play an important role in determining an object's base height.

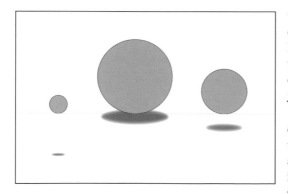

When the base of a shadow makes contact with the base of our sprite, we know that the object is grounded, giving precedence to base height in our perception of the scene. Then, when the shadows are absent, we may be uncertain as to whether we can assume the object is in contact with the ground.

At those times when an object is not in contact with the ground, the shadow will establish a base height for which we can once again compare the depths of objects. This is evident in Figure 6.11 in which the three spheres have the same base height, yet the locations of the shadows indicate clearly that the largest object is farthest from the camera.

Figure 6.11. Depth principle 2: base height from shadows.

6.3.3 Scale

The third and perhaps most obvious principle of depth is *scale*. The greater the distance an object is from the view point, the smaller it appears. In Figure 6.12 we can see that scale can be very effective when combined with base height. In this image we also get our first glimpse at traditional perspective drawing: guide lines indicate both a vanishing point and a horizon line.

Figure 6.12. Depth principle 3: scale with base height.

However, even without the help of base height, scale is an effective indicator of distance when we can assume that the objects we are comparing would otherwise be equivalent in size. Figure 6.13 shows an example of this, as there are no consistent visual cues other than the relative scale of the balloons and our expectations of the balloons' actual sizes.

Figure 6.12 is an example of the monocular cue called *relative size*, whereas Figure 6.13 is an example of *familiar size*.

Figure 6.13. Depth principle 3: scale.

Figure 6.14. Depth principle 4: the effect of atmosphere on the distant hills along the Alaskan Highway. (Photograph by John Pile Jr.)

6.3.4 Atmosphere

A fourth and often overlooked principle of distance, especially for objects a significant distance from the camera, is the effect that *atmosphere* has on the object being rendered. The best way to demonstrate this effect is by looking at actual photographs (or even just looking out the window). In the photo shown in Figure 6.14, note the crisp colors of the foreground objects and how they compare to the colors of the distant hills.

This dulling of colors is due to the fact that as the photons of light make their way across the valley, they are scattered as they interact with the molecules in the air. Combining the complexity of the various wavelengths of visible light with the various particles that may exist in the air at any point, distant objects may appear dulled, darkened, hidden, or otherwise have their natural color obscured by the atmosphere. The term for this monocular cue is *aerial perspective*.

This effect can be seen in the painting in Figure 6.1 at the beginning of this chapter. Note how the most distant columns of the aqueduct are lighter than the nearest ones. These atmospheric effects may be intensified during rain, snow, or fog. The effect is even more apparent when the objects are lit only by a localized light source.

6.3.5 Focus

When the *focus* of a lens is on a particular object, objects at other distances may be out of focus. Most often, 2D games assume an infinite viewing distance (as with isometric tiled graphics). However, if we want to emphasize the depth of a scene or when we want to focus the player's attention on a particular layer of depth, it may be appropriate to blur objects that are not important to game play and are very close or very far away from the most important action.

We saw this principle earlier in the chapter in Figure 6.4. The snowmen in the foreground were purposely blurred to make them appear out of focus.

Since we should assume the image is naturally in focus, a more appropriate term for application of this principle to outlying objects would be *defocus blur*.

6.3.6 Parallax

A final and regularly used principle of depth is called *parallax*. Fundamentally, the concept is the same as that described for scale. That is, objects that are farther away appear to be smaller. However, what makes it a separate principle is that we can also scale motion.

Specifically, if the scale of an object appears to be at half its normal size, it should also appear to move at half the speed. For example, assume we are animating a scene in which the sprite of a car (20 pixels wide) moves across the screen. On a 1:1 scale, assume that the vehicle is now moving at 10 pixels per frame (half a car length), when rendered in the distance at half the scale, the vehicle should now cover only 5 pixels per frame.

While this adds a nice realistic effect, the real visual magic happens when we apply this same concept to inanimate objects and combine it with a panning camera. As the camera moves to the right, objects will appear to move to the left at a rate proportional to their relative scale. In Figure 6.15, at each frame the snowmen move one unit to the left, but the unit size is relative to their scale. The result is a scene that pans correctly.

The first significant application of this technique on a large scale was achieved through Disney's multi-

Figure 6.15. Depth Principle 6: Parallax. From top to bottom, as the camera moves to the right the game object appear to move to the left at a rate proportional to their distance.

plane camera. Through the use of a camera vertically positioned above multiple layers of background images painted onto sheets of glass, the Disney animators could render moving backgrounds, which would move at the appropriate speed based on the rules of parallax [Disney 57]. As mentioned initially, this is not just limited to the relative motion of the static background objects but should also be applied to objects moving within these layers.

However, applying the effect of parallax on very distant object (for example, a mountain range that is 100 miles away) means that these objects appear to be completely static in relation to a moving background. Any object that we would consider infinitely far away should be held static when the camera pans from side to side as well as when the camera zooms in and out. That is, we assume the zoom of the camera is meant to simulate a camera that is moving forward into the scene.

This is another feature of Disney's multiplane camera. It would allow the animators to zoom into a scene while correctly holding the most distant objects at the correct scale. This illusion of a camera moving into what would otherwise be a flat image can be seen most dramatically in the opening scene of Disney's *Beauty and the Beast* [Disney 91], in which the camera moves through a very stylized forest.

6.3.7 Additional Monocular Cues

Through these six principles of depth, we have covered what I consider to be the most important monocular cues for use in programming our game. However, there are others.

We have already noted how the location of shadows can play a role in understanding the depth of an object; however, lighting and shading can have a much more significant effect than just helping us understand the relative distance of objects. The shape of the shadows in Figure 6.11 indicates the geometric shape of the object. In this case, the shadows indicated that each blue circle is a sphere instead of a flat disc or the blunt end of cylinder.

Additionally, shadows on objects help to define the shape of the object. In the snowmen in Figure 6.7, the curved shaded region on the bottom-left defines the spherical curve to the base of the snowman. In each of these cases, these are subtle details best left to a 2D artist.

Another cue, also best left to the artist, is the fact that fine detail becomes difficult to see when viewed at a distance. Sometimes referred to as *texture gradient*, it might be easiest to understand by considering a concrete surface. When the surface is close to the viewer, the texture of the concrete become very apparent, but at a distance, the detail is lost.

A final monocular cue is *curvilinear perspective*, the apparent curve of parallel lines as they reach the edge of our vision or when viewed through a fisheye lens.

6.4   The Six Principles in Code

Now let's look at a very simple way of implementing these six principles of depth in code. To keep things simple, let's start with a basic animated character similar to the one created in Section 4.2 in which the running boy is drawn on screen. The following code samples make use of a runner class that contains all the information necessary to draw the runner, similar to the sprite class defined earlier.

Specifically, this new runner class has the following structure:

```
1   class cRunner
    {
      //Source Data
      private Texture2D m_tSrcSpriteSheet;
5     private Rectangle m_rSrcLocation;
      private Vector2 m_vSrcOrigin;

      //Destination Data
      public Vector2 m_vPos;
10    public Color m_cDestColor;
      public float m_fDestRotation;
      public float m_fDestScale;
      public float m_fDestDepth;
      public SpriteEffects m_eDestSprEff;

15
      //Animation Data
      private int m_iCurrentCel;
      private int m_iNumberOfCels;
      private int m_iMsUntilNextCel;
20    private int m_iMsPerCel;

      public bool m_bIsRunning;

      public cRunner()...

25
      public void Initialize()
      {
        m_fDestRotation = 0.0f;
        m_fDestScale = 1.0f;
30      m_rSrcLocation = new Rectangle(0, 0, 128, 128);
        m_vSrcOrigin = Vector.Zero();
      }

      public void LoadContent(ContentManager pContent, String
          fileName)
```

```
35   {
       m_tSrcSpriteSheet = pContent.Load<Texture2D>(fileName);
     }

     public void Update(GameTime gameTime)
40   {
       UpdateAnimation(gameTime);
       m_fDestDepth = 1.0f;
     }

45   public void Draw(SpriteBatch pBatch)...

     private void UpdateAnimation(GameTime gameTime)...

   }
```

The definitions for the longer functions should be fairly obvious by now.
However, if you need help, see the following:

```
1    public cRunner()
     {
       m_cDestColor = Color.White;
       m_eDestSprEff = SpriteEffects.None;
5
       m_iNumberOfCels = 12;
       m_iCurrentCel = 0;
       m_iMsPerCel = 50;
       m_iMsUntilNextCel = m_iMsPerCel;
10   }

     public void Draw(SpriteBatch pBatch)
     {
       pBatch.Draw(m_tSrcSpriteSheet,
15     m_vPos,
       m_rSrcLocation,
       m_cDestColor,
       m_fDestRotation,
       m_vSrcOrigin,
20     m_fDestScale,
       m_eDestSprEff,
       m_fDestDepth);
     }

25   private void UpdateAnimation(GameTime gameTime)
     {
       m_iMsUntilNextCel -= gameTime.ElapsedGameTime.
          Milliseconds;

       if ((m_iMsUntilNextCel <= 0) && (m_bIsRunning))
30     {
         m_iCurrentCel++;
         m_iMsUntilNextCel = m_iMsPerCel;
       }
```

```
35    if (m_iCurrentCel >= m_iNumberOfCels)
          m_iCurrentCel = 0;

      m_rSrcLocation.X = m_rSrcLocation.Width * m_iCurrentCel;
    }

40
  }
```

Then in the game code, all we need is something like the following:

```
1  //Member Functions:
   cRunner runner;

   //In Constructor:
5  //...
   graphics = new GraphicsDeviceManager(this);
   graphics.PreferredBackBufferWidth = 1280;
   graphics.PreferredBackBufferHeight = 720;
   Content.RootDirectory = "Content";
10 runner = new cRunner();


   //In Initialize Function:
   runner.Initialize();
15 runner.m_vPos = new Vector2(400, 400);


   //In LoadContent Function:
   runner.LoadContent(Content, "run\_cycle");
20

   //In Update Function:
   runner.m_bIsRunning = false;

25 if (Keyboard.GetState().IsKeyDown(Keys.Up))
   {
       runner.m_bIsRunning = true;
       runner.m_vPos.Y -= 3;
   }
30 else if (Keyboard.GetState().IsKeyDown(Keys.Down))
   {
       runner.m_bIsRunning = true;
       runner.m_vPos.Y += 3;
   }
35
   if (Keyboard.GetState().IsKeyDown(Keys.Left))
   {
       runner.m_eDestSprEff = SpriteEffects.FlipHorizontally;
       runner.m_bIsRunning = true;
40     runner.m_vPos.X -= 5;
   }
   else if (Keyboard.GetState().IsKeyDown(Keys.Right))
   {
       runner.m_eDestSprEff = SpriteEffects.None;
```

```
45        runner.m_bIsRunning = true;
          runner.m_vPos.X += 5;
      }
      runner.Update(gameTime);

50
      //In Draw Function:
      //...
      spriteBatch.Begin(SpriteSortMode.FrontToBack, BlendState.
          NonPremultiplied);
      runner.Draw(spriteBatch);
55    spriteBatch.End();
      //...
```

6.4.1   Base Height

It makes sense to start with the concept of base height first. We already track a sprite's position in x-y coordinates, so we just need to ensure that the origin of the sprite is located at the base of the figure on the sprite. For the runner sprite, the base texel occurs at about $(57, 105)$.

In that case, you'll need to update the source origin in the cRunner class initialization as follows:

```
1    m_vSrcOrigin = new Vector2(57, 105);
```

6.4.2   Overlap

In order to get overlap to work correctly, we use the XNA depth value and make use of the principle of base height. That is, the lower the y-value of the destination position, the lower the depth value should be. XNA requires that we track a depth value between 0 and 1, so our equation might look like the following:

$$\text{depth} = \frac{y\text{-position}}{\text{screen height}}.$$

The result would give us a value from 0 to 1, where 0 indicates the sprite is at the top of the screen and thus farthest from view and 1 indicates the sprite is at the bottom of the screen and thus closest to view.

The end result will look much better, however, if we create a horizon line and modify the equation as follows, which will provide a depth value such that the 0 is aligned with the horizon line:

$$\text{depth} = \frac{y\text{-position}-\text{horizon}}{\text{screen height}-\text{horizon}}.$$

The value for the line should match the horizon line in any background image. However, without a background image, in this example we can simply set the horizon to an arbitrary but appropriate value, say $y = 240$ (one-third the way down a 720-pixel-high screen).

In the runner class, we create a new function and modify the update function to make use of the new function:

```
public int m_cHorizon = 240;

public void UpdateDepth(GameTime gameTime)
{
    m_fDestDepth = (m_vPos.Y - m_cHorizon) / (720 - m_cHorizon)
        ;
}

public void Update(GameTime gameTime)
{
    UpdateAnimation(gameTime);
    UpdateDepth(gameTime);
}
```

This code makes the assumption that the player will never have a y-axis position value less than the horizon value. We need to add that limitation to the game's Update function, just after checking for keyboard input. In XNA, we can use the MathHelper.Clamp function.

```
//In Game Update:

//...
runner.m_vPos.Y = MathHelper.Clamp(runner.m_vPos.Y, runner.
    m_cHorizon, 720);
runner.Update(gameTime);
//...
```

Of course, none of this will be visible unless we have something for the character to overlap. In this case, we can quickly create a second instance of the runner class. We won't worry about moving or animating the second runner for now.

Be sure to add the following in the appropriate locations of your game:

```
//Member variables
cRunner runner2;

//Constructor
runner2 = new cRunner();

//Initialize
runner2.Initialize();
runner2.m_vPos = new Vector2(600, 400);

//Load Content:
runner2.LoadContent(Content, "run_cycle");
```

```
     //Update:
15   runner2.Update(gameTime);

     //Draw:
     runner2.Draw(spriteBatch);
```

Figure 6.16. Base height and overlap applied to sprites.

Your two runners should now be layered and interact appropriately. You should now have no trouble taking this a step further, creating a snowman class and randomly placing snowmen throughout the scene. Be sure to define the snowman sprite's origin appropriately.

By adding a background image, you should get something similar to Figure 6.16, in which I have added 25 randomly placed snowmen.

6.4.3 Scale

To add the scale principle, we need to decide the minimum scaling value we are willing to use in our game. In this case, let's assume that when a sprite is as close to the viewer as possible, its scale is 1.0 and, when a sprite is standing on the horizon line, its scale is 25% of its original size. We can then linearly calculate all other values by making use of the depth value, which already gives us a value between 0 and 1:

$$scale = 0.25 + (depth \times 0.75).$$

Once again, create a function to update the scale and be sure to add a call in the Update function of the runner class.

```
1    public void UpdateScale(GameTime gameTime)
     {
        m_fDestScale = 0.25f + (m_fDestDepth * 0.75f);
     }

5
     public void Update(GameTime gameTime)
     {
        UpdateAnimation(gameTime);
        UpdateDepth(gameTime);
10      UpdateScale(gameTime);
     }
```

The result of scaling based on depth is fairly dramatic, as can be seen in Figure 6.17.

Once again, remember that the decision to scale your sprites should be done with care. You can see significant degradation in the quality of the smallest snowmen in Figure 6.17 as a result of real-time scaling of the sprite. You may want to limit the amount of scaling you apply to your sprites or use a prescaled sprite when the scaling is significant. In 3D graphics, with a technique called mipmapping (see Section 3.4.2), the graphics card selects the most appropriately sized texture to use from a series of prescaled textures. Using a mipmapping technique when scaling greatly improves the quality of the final image.

Figure 6.17. Adding the principle of scale to sample code.

6.4.4 Atmosphere

To create an atmospheric effect, we are somewhat limited in what we can achieve with sprites and the sprite batch. By using the color parameter, we can make a sprite darker, but it is not necessarily an easy task to render a sprite at a lighter color. Let's start by looking at a possibility for rendering distant objects slightly darker than nearer objects.

As before, we come up with a linear relationship between the objects based on their depth. In this case, it is the color of the object that will be modified.

```
public void UpdateColor(GameTime gameTime)
{
   float greyValue = 0.75f + (m_fDestDepth * 0.25f);
   m_cDestColor = new Color(greyValue, greyValue, greyValue);
}

public void Update(GameTime gameTime)
{
   UpdateAnimation(gameTime);
   UpdateDepth(gameTime);
   UpdateScale(gameTime);
   UpdateColor(gameTime);
}
```

The result is an image in which the closest sprites are drawn with RGB values of 1.0, and the sprites on the horizon are drawn with RGB values of 0.75 (see Figure 6.18). Even though this does create an atmospheric effect,

Figure 6.18. Atmospheric effect with darkening.

Figure 6.19. Atmospheric effect with alpha blend.

it would be more appropriate for a night scene in which the farthest sprites blend into the darkness.

Instead, you might be tempted to use the alpha value. Using an alpha blend does create a nice effect of fading to white, but only when there is no overlap occurring. When two sprites overlap, the result is a seemingly translucent sprite, as seen in Figure 6.19.

In order to achieve a better fade-to-white effect, we will need to apply advanced graphics techniques that we have not yet covered. Come back to this section after completing Chapter 9, which will help you find a solution to the problem.

6.4.5   Focus

Dynamically blurring out-of-focus sprites is another principle that must wait until we have discussed advanced graphical techniques. Just as for fade-to-white, Chapter 9 will help you to create a pixel shader that will achieve the desired result.

6.4.6   Parallax

Finally, parallax is not difficult to build into our game. The easiest way to achieve parallax is to distinguish the difference between the sprite's position in the game and where it appears to be located on the screen. Then scale the player's display position based on the previously calculated scale by using

$$\text{draw position } (x\text{-value}) = \text{game position } (x\text{-value}) \times \text{scale}.$$

However, before we can do this, let's make sure we are using a combination of velocities and positions. Since we want to move at various rates, depending on how far away we are from the camera, using velocities will help ensure we understand how this is all working.

First, we update our input to use velocity values, measured in pixels per second.

```
//Game Update Function:

if (Keyboard.GetState().IsKeyDown(Keys.Up))
{
    runner.m_vVel.Y -= 10f;
}
else if (Keyboard.GetState().IsKeyDown(Keys.Down))
```

```
        {
            runner.m_vVel.Y += 10f;
10      }

        if (Keyboard.GetState().IsKeyDown(Keys.Left))
        {
            runner.m_eDestSprEff = SpriteEffects.FlipHorizontally;
15          runner.m_vVel.X -= 10f;
        }
        else if (Keyboard.GetState().IsKeyDown(Keys.Right))
        {
            runner.m_eDestSprEff = SpriteEffects.None;
20          runner.m_vVel.X += 10f;
        }
```

Notice the new value of `m_vVel`. We need to add this velocity to the runner class.

```
1   //Game Data
    public Vector2 m_vVel;
    public Vector2 m_vPos;
```

We then need to make the link between the position and the velocity. As just mentioned, the velocity is now a measurement of pixels per second. To ensure that this value is accurate, in every frame we modify the position by the velocity proportional to the number of seconds that has elapsed since the last frame.

We also need a maximum velocity. This can be calculated by considering the maximum speed for pixels to move across the frame. Let's use 6.0 seconds for a sprite to move across the screen that is 1280 pixels wide.

Note that the y-position clamp has also moved into this same function.

```
1   public void UpdatePosition(GameTime gameTime)
    {
        float MAX_VEL = 1280 / 6.0f;

5       m_vVel *= 0.95f;  //friction
        m_vVel.X = MathHelper.Clamp(m_vVel.X, -MAX_VEL, +MAX_VEL);
        m_vVel.Y = MathHelper.Clamp(m_vVel.Y, -MAX_VEL, +MAX_VEL);

        m_vPos.X += (float)(m_vVel.X * gameTime.ElapsedGameTime.
            TotalSeconds);
10      m_vPos.Y += (float)(m_vVel.Y * gameTime.ElapsedGameTime.
            TotalSeconds);
        m_vPos.Y = MathHelper.Clamp(m_vPos.Y, m_cHorizon, 720);
    }

    public void Update(GameTime gameTime)
15  {
        UpdatePosition(gameTime);
        UpdateAnimation(gameTime);
        UpdateDepth(gameTime);
```

```
          UpdateScale(gameTime);
20        UpdateColor(gameTime);
      }
```

We need to add the new draw position. As before, we also add a camera
location in order to keep the view centered on the player. However, this
time we limit the camera movement to the x-axis.

```
1   public void Draw(SpriteBatch pBatch, Vector2 pCameraLocation)
    {
      Vector2 m_vDrawPos = m_vPos;
      m_vDrawPos.X -= (pCameraLocation.X);
5     m_vDrawPos.X += (1280/2);        //Camera Offset

      pBatch.Draw(m_tSrcSpriteSheet,
        m_vDrawPos,                    //previously m_vPos,
        m_rSrcLocation,
10        m_cDestColor,
        m_fDestRotation,
        m_vSrcOrigin,
        m_fDestScale,
        m_eDestSprEff,
15        m_fDestDepth);
    }
```

Finally, in the game class, we add the camera position tracking and
modify the Draw call to use the camera location.

```
1   protected override void Draw(GameTime gameTime)
    {
      GraphicsDevice.Clear(Color.White);

5     cameraLocation = new Vector2(runner.m_vPos.X, 0.0f);

      spriteBatch.Begin(SpriteSortMode.FrontToBack, BlendState.
          NonPremultiplied);

      //Draw background image
10      //...

      //Draw runners
      runner.Draw(spriteBatch, cameraLocation);
      runner2.Draw(spriteBatch, cameraLocation);
15
      //Draw other game sprites
          //...

      spriteBatch.End();
20
      base.Draw(gameTime);
    }
```

With those modifications we are ready to add parallax to the scene. As noted, we simply scale the x-value based on the sprite's calculated depth value. We do this after adjusting for the camera location but before adjusting for the camera offset in the Draw function of the camera class.

```
public void Draw(SpriteBatch pBatch, Vector2 pCameraLocation)
{
    Vector2 m_vDrawPos = m_vPos;
    m_vDrawPos.X -= (pCameraLocation.X);
    m_vDrawPos.X *= m_fDestScale;
    m_vDrawPos.X += (1280/2);      //Camera Offset

    //...
}
```

Figures 6.20 and 6.21 show the difference in scaled position due to parallax. Another important thing to note in the parallax before and after images is that although the snowmen are evenly spaced, they are not correctly scaled in the y-direction. This is because the we have based all the depth calculations on y-position.

An easy solution would be to ensure that as a sprite moves, we scale the motion in the y-direction. This can be accomplished in the position update function in the runner class.

Figure 6.20. Before applying parallax, the distant snowmen are spread evenly across the x-axis.

```
//m_vPos.Y += (float)(m_vVel.Y * gameTime.ElapsedGameTime.
    TotalSeconds);
m_vPos.Y += (float)(m_fDestScale * m_vVel.Y * gameTime.
    ElapsedGameTime.TotalSeconds);
```

This will fix relative movement, ensuring that motion away from the camera is scaled. However, this is not a very good solution because it requires that we adjust for the drawing scale when setting initial positions of objects in the game world. Since it is possible that the drawing scale may change during game development, it would be better to have a solution that scaled the y-axis appropriately. This is a challenge presented at the end of this chapter

Figure 6.21. After applying parallax, the distant snowmen are scaled evenly across the x-axis based on their depth.

6.5   Traditional Perspective

By themselves, the six principles of depth are only parts a much broader topic. They describe individual visual effects, but not the traditional artistic rules that have developed over the last half millennium for ensuring that these rules are applied correctly.

As a brief introduction to the traditional perspective, we consider three concepts when applying the six principles of depth: vanishing point, horizon, and eye level.

6.5.1   Vanishing Point

Consider a straight road as it heads into the distance, as in Figure 6.24. In the image, the *vanishing point* is that location where the lines of the road merge to become a single pixel. This type of single-point linear perspective is a common starting point for beginning artists to explore the concepts of perspective. In more advanced types of perspective, multiple vanishing points may be used.

These points are used by the artist as guideline when placing objects and ensuring they are the correct size. We have a significant advantage in that we are not restricted to the traditional rules governing vanishing points and perspectives. This is because we can use code to appropriately size our sprites by using mathematical equations instead of basing the scale on guidelines. It is important to work closely with the artist to ensure that our equations are appropriate for the particular background and art assets for the game.

6.5.2   Horizon

Figure 6.22. Horizon.

A common definition of *horizon* might be "a horizontal line representing the intersection of sky and earth when viewed from a particular location" (see Figure 6.22).

For our purposes, it is tempting to think of the horizon as the point on the y-axis at which the scale of the game objects become zero. In other words, we get an infinite set of vanishing points, defined by the Cartesian coordinates, of all the x-values at a given y-value. This is the general rule we applied in our code examples earlier in this chapter. However, this is not always true and occurs only when the vanishing points are actually located on the horizon line, as would be the case when standing on an infinite flat terrain looking out horizontally.

In the real world, the relationship between the horizon line and the vanishing points is only an approximation. There are plenty of examples in which it is easy to see that the vanishing points are not actually located on the horizon. For example, when standing on a beach and looking out across the ocean, we know that the curvature of Earth causes a ship to disappear beyond the horizon before it has a scale that is too small to be seen. Another example involves looking up from the bottom of a hill. The actual horizon line may be obscured, but we may have an artificial horizon line apparent from many objects located on the constant slope. In an opposite example, the camera may be looking downhill, as shown in Figure 6.23.

Figure 6.23. Looking down a sloped terrain with a horizon in the distance. The short marks on either side of the image represent the artificial horizon line for the objects on the slope.

However, it is unlikely that these limitations will be an issue in our games. Game play is often limited to an area significantly closer than the horizon, and it is unlikely that your artist and designers will create a 2D game that occurs on a significant slope. If they do, however, you should now be able to create an appropriate framework that is close enough. You will have to deal with the limitations of scaling raster graphics before you will need to worry about the discrepancy between the horizon line and vanishing points.

6.5.3 Eye Level

The final important aspect to perspective is *eye level*. We might be better off to consider this as the camera height. In any case, eye level is an important aspect of perspective that helps our mind to understand the relative height of the objects in the scene.

As you can see in Figure 6.24(a), the boy's eyes are aligned to the horizon line. Because of this, we know that the camera is at the same relative height from the ground as the boy's eyes. We also know that since the eyes of the snowman are aligned above the horizon line, the snowman is both taller than the boy and taller than the viewer.

In Figure 6.24(b), the horizon line is aligned with the snowman's eyes. In this case we know that the viewer is roughly the same height as the snowmen as well as taller than the boy.

(a)

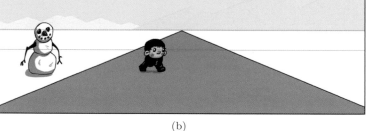

(b)

Figure 6.24. (a) Boy's eye level at the horizon. (b) Snowman's eye level at the horizon.

More generally, this tells us that on level terrain, any distant object with a height that does not cross the horizon line is shorter than the viewer. This is an important tool in helping us create an appropriate scale, and it is something to consider in your application.

Let us now re-examine our depth code from earlier. Recall that in Section 6.4.3 we used the following rather arbitrary values for calculating scale:

$$\text{scale} = 0.25 + (\text{depth} \times 0.75).$$

To take a more exact approach, suppose now we want to ensure that the camera is located at the same height as the snowman eye level. On the sprite sheet, the distance from the snowman's eye level to the snowman's base is approximately 135 pixels. Taking into account from our knowledge of perspective that the horizon should be aligned with the eye level of the snowman, we can calculate the appropriate scale of the snowman whose base is located at the very bottom of the screen:

$$\text{maximum scale} = \frac{\text{screen height–horizon height}}{\text{snowman base–snowman eye level}}.$$

Figure 6.25. Snowman's eye level.

Figure 6.26. Runner's eye level.

At the same time, we can see that the distance from the runner's eye level to its base on the sprite sheet is about 70 pixels. So replacing the scale calculation, we could use something like the following. In either case, we simply set the eye level to match that of the sprite with which we want to align.

```
public void UpdateScale(GameTime gameTime)
{
    float fEyeLevel = 70.0f;        //runner
    //float fEyeLevel = 135.0f;     //snowman
    m_fDestScale = m_fDestDepth * ((720.0f - m_cHorizon) /
        fEyeLevel);
}
```

The results of switching between these two eye levels can be seen in Figures 6.25 and 6.26.

6.5.4 False Perspective

It is important to note the results of the incorrect application of the basic rules of perspective. We can mix and match a variety of techniques, but if the scene as a whole does not apply perspective correctly and consistently, the results could be absurd (see Figure 6.27).

But we are making games that don't necessarily have to fit reality. As we have already noted, a variety of games do not scale the sprites as they move forward and backward. Given the stylized nature of the graphics and the benefit of artistic license, the results of this lack of scale are rarely noticed by the player.

However, we could take this even further. By purposely creating a false perspective, we may end up with a unique game play that takes the work of artists such as Rob Gonsalves, Giovanni Piranesi, or M. C. Escher to an interactive level. I encourage you to play with perspective and false perspective within your 2D games.

Figure 6.27. *Satire on False Perspective* by William Hogarth, 1753. The caption reads: "Whoever makes a design without the knowledge of perspective will be liable to such absurdities as are shewn in this frontispiece" (from a book on linear perspective by John Joshua Kirby) [Kirby 54].

6.6   Summary

A variety of tools help us to create the illusion of depth in our 2D games. The six principles of depth offer a foundation for building the type of system that can help your artist and possibly offer some new and interesting game play.

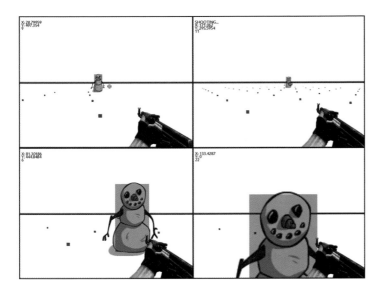

Figure 6.28. Gunther Fox's 2.5D prototype, 2010.

One of the best examples from film of applying the illusion of depth to a 2D image can be found in the "Circle of Life" opening of Disney's *The Lion King* [Disney 94]. During this sequence, the animators repeatedly apply the techniques covered in this chapter in an attempt to demonstrate the depth of the images. How many can you count?

After going through these topics with my class in 2010, one of my students took the six basic principles and built a first-person shooter using only 2D sprites and the simple math we have listed above. In Gunther Fox's prototype (see Figure 6.28), he applied the additional math for moving and rotating the camera within the game world. While this is not the method I would advise for anyone wanting to work in three dimensions, Fox's prototype does show the ability to take 2D to an extreme.

Exercises: Challenges

Challenge 6.1. Analyze a 2D game or animated film looking for a scene with an interesting perspective. Create a game prototype making use of the same perspective, allowing the character to navigate within the scene in a believable way.

Challenge 6.2. The examples in this chapter were limited to objects that rest on the ground. Now add the ability to have the player jump.

Hint: You'll need to use an "offset height" in your jump calculation, applied in a way that will ensure the sprite scale does not shrink as the player jumps into the air. At the same time, the jump height should be scaled appropriately based on the current depth.

Challenge 6.3. Replace the runner class with an animated sprite class derived from a sprite class.

Challenge 6.4. Redesign the parallax code to scale the y-axis appropriately. Give the user the ability to change the values that determine the parallax scale while the game is running.

Chapter 7

User Interface

A graphics programmer's job does not end at rendering the in-game world. A large amount of work is required to develop menus, interfaces, and other on-screen feedback to players, programmers, and testers.

The reality is that the user interface (UI) can be as important to the player's experience as the game itself. Giordano Contestabile, director of the team that developed *Bejewled Blitz* stressed the importance of the user interface at a 2012 Game Developer Conference: "Don't let UI be an afterthought. Hire a great UI designer and empower them to make decisions. Put them at the management table" [Contestabile 12].

This chapter looks at different types of UIs, addresses multiple-language support, and explores the UI expectations of game publishers.

7.1 UI Types

7.1.1 Overlay

As mentioned above, the UI choice can have a surprisingly significant effect on the gamer's experience. On the one extreme are flight simulators and racing games that implement a complete cockpit, full of realistic gauges, in an attempt to put the player "in the driver's seat." As a result there is a clear boundary between the game-play world (out there) and the cockpit (in here). Often this is taken a step further by simulating the existence of a window that may occasionally be splashed with splotches of mud or dotted with pools of raindrops. In the extreme, the play may even see the interior of a fighter pilot's helmet or an American football helmet guard (although I can't think of any examples where this has been done).

On the other extreme is the minimalist foreground used in *Thief* [Looking Glass Studios 98]. In this game, Warren Spector's stated goal was to completely immerse the player into the game. He did not want the feeling that anything was between the player and the environment. All that was included was a tiny inventory menu that would quickly disappear from view when unused and a small light meter to indicate how well the player was concealed by shadows.

In both extremes, the game view is represented by a first-person perspective, but it is the foreground (or lack there of) that determines the depth of the game play. Somewhere in between is the situation of needing a great deal of information displayed to the player, but with the goal of not adding the layer of abstraction that is achieved with a full cockpit. In these cases, the concepts (and terminology) are borrowed directly from military aircraft, that is, the use of a ***heads-up display*** (HUD). In the physical aircraft, the image is shown in a way that only the necessary information is displayed superimposed over the pilot's view. In many cases, the term HUD has become synonymous with any GUI presented in the foreground.

A more typical GUI for the third-person perspective is the atypical role-playing game (RPG) foreground, made standard with the release of *Diablo* [Blizzard North 96], consisting of health and mana orbs or a similar type of percentage-depleted gauge, an inventory that can be hidden from view, and a set of buttons representing quick access skills. The more information that is displayed, the more the game play is hidden from view. Whether intentional or not, this type of GUI sends a clear message to the player that the avatar is there in the game world and the player is separate, detached from that action. Again, it is the depth created by the foreground that creates a layer of abstraction.

As a side note, an interesting twist on this type of game play layered by a foreground is found, for example, in *Guitar Hero* [Harmonix 05], in which the GUI is the game play. The background may consist of a fully rendered 3D environment, but it is irrelevant to the game play.

7.2 Fonts

7.2.1 Font Sprite Sheet

In some cases, the library or framework you are utilizing to build your game may come with built-in fonts. In other cases, or in the cases for which the built-in fonts are not sufficient, you may want to create your own font as a combination of sprites.

In these cases, just as easily as a sprite sheet contains individual sprites, a ***font sprite sheet*** (with bitmap fonts) can contain all the individual letters that make up your desired font (see the example in Figure 7.1). The order of these can be made to match the ASCII value of the characters for ease of use.

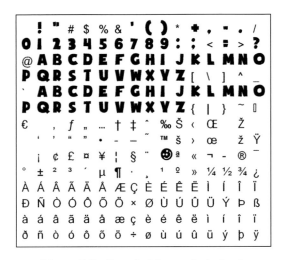

In addition to the location of each sprite, you also want to track the width of each letter. For example, the letter W will require more pixels than the letter i. A variety of freely available programs (bitmap font generators) exist that will allow you to create a sprite sheet of fonts. In addition to the final image, these programs will also create a text file with a list of letter width information.

Figure 7.1. Sample bitmap font sheet.

7.2.2   Sprite Fonts in XNA

Using XNA, creating and working with fonts becomes frighteningly easy. Not only does the framework automatically convert any TrueType font for use in your game, a host of library files allow you to work with the text.

A *spritefont* file is created in the content folder and consists of an XML definition of the font settings (name, size, spacing, style, etc.). Then, the content pipeline in XNA converts the TrueType font into an asset that is usable within your game.

Assuming a spritefont file in your content folder called fontDefinition .spritefont exists, you can then load the spritefont as follows:

```
public SpriteFont myFont;

//In LoadContent:

Content.Load<SpriteFont>("fontDefinition");
```

Rendering the spritefont is similar to rendering any other sprite, only we will now use the DrawString function. Otherwise, it will act just like the Draw function, requiring location, scale, rotation, and other values.

```
spriteBatch.Begin();
spriteBatch.DrawString(myFont, "Hello World", /* ... */ );
spriteBatch.End();
```

In addition to the ability to easily generate spritefonts through the XNA content pipeline, XNA also has a set of useful spritefont manipulation tools. These allow you to measure the pixel width of a string for ease in text alignment. For example, the following code centers the text on the screen.

```
1   String myString = "Hello World";
    Vector2 size = myFont.MeasureString(myString);
    Vector2 centeredLoc = new Vector2((1280 / 2) - (size.X / 2),
                                       (720 / 2) - (size.Y / 2));
5
    spriteBatch.Begin();
    spriteBatch.DrawString(myFont, myString, centeredLoc, Color.
        Black);
    spriteBatch.End();
```

7.3   Localization

Localization is the process of converting your game for use in other regions. It is important to note that there are slight differences even among English-speaking countries; the most significant localization task is converting from one language to another. Although this might not seem like a job for the graphics programmer, the truth is that the conversion from one language to another often results in significant changes to the layout of your game UI.

Figure 7.2. Localization: overlap issues.

The most common example is the issue faced when converting from English to German. The German language is notorious among game developers because the German translations often contain far more letters (and thus screen space) than the original English. The result is overlapping text (see Figure 7.2) or text that is rendered outside the screen.

As the graphics programmer, you need to come up with a solution for such issues. You may be tempted to simply render the text at a smaller scale, but it is likely that this would lead to unreadable text at certain resolutions. More robust solutions may be required, by first wrapping and then dynamically scrolling the text in a particular text window.

However, before you start designing your graphical UI solution, you should implement a localization plan that allows you to change languages while the game is running for debugging purposes (perhaps by pressing a secret key combination). The more common (and ill-advised) solution is to load a single language at the start of the game. This means that in order to test your game in various languages, you need to restart the game. Imagine the worst-case scenario in which you have to play through the entire game in order to test that the new language layout is correct in the end-game sequence.

Ideally, at any point in the game, you should be able to cycle through the various languages to make sure they all *look* correct, even if you can't read what they say.

Of course, this assumes that all on-screen text is stored in a look-up table such as a dictionary or other data structure. It is very important to never (even in the early stages of game development) hard-code text strings. If you do, you may spend hours searching for the text when you want to edit it later. The best solution is to read all your text from a file so that it is in a single location and can easily be edited without requiring you to recompile the code.

7.3.1 Other Localizations

In many cases, it's not only the language itself that is different. In parts of Europe, the symbols used for numeric representation are quite different from those used in the United States and United Kingdom. For example, in the United States, large numbers are separated by commas, as in 1,234,567, whereas in Europe the same number may be written as 1.234.456. Conversely, in the United States $1/4 = 0.25$, instead of the European $1/4 = 0,25$.

Another common issue concerns dates. The United States has a preference for the "month day, year" format, but in most of the rest of the world the format is "day month year." This might not be an issue when written out, but it definitely is an issue when using the numeric notation DD-MM-YYYY compared with MM-DD-YYYY.

None of these are serious issues in themselves, but it is important to note the differences and plan for them in your localization. With digital distribution, the reach of our games becomes global, and you don't want simple localization mistakes to frustrate or alienate your audience.

7.3.2 Special Characters

In designing for other languages, there may be cases when your font does not have sufficient characters—for example, when converting to use the Cyrillic letters of the Russian languages. In these cases, it may be necessary for your artist to add characters in your bitmap font.

In other cases, it may be important to note cultural significance in the language. For example, in Japan the cross button (what we might call the X button) on the PlayStation console is swapped with the circle button. In Japan, the concept of "press X to continue" does not make sense because the cultural significance is that the cross is equivalent to "stop."

7.3.3　Platform-Specific Localization

Figure 7.3. Platform-specific localization: press A to continue.

In addition to these international issues, it is likely that for clarity (and it is often required by a publisher), you will need to place graphics of the buttons inline (see Figure 7.3) or other system features in place of the letters or descriptions. For example, an up arrow may have to be overlaid on an image of the direction pad instead of simply writing "press up."

7.4　Safe Frames

When building the user interface, it is important to ensure that all vital information is visible on the screen. This is not usually an issue when deploying games to the PC or mobile devices, but it *is* common for the inside border around a television to obscure the edges of the screen.

Knowing that this is a likely possibility, important game information is commonly kept within a smaller frame of the screen, called the *safe frame* (see Figure 7.4). The valid unsafe range varies by console manufacturer, but it can be as much as the outer 15 percent of the screen. Planning for this early in the game development phase will ensure you don't end up with issues later.

Therefore, you should align your text with the edges of the safe frame. Further, while testing your game, it may be useful to create an overlay so that anything outside the safe frame is immediately obvious.

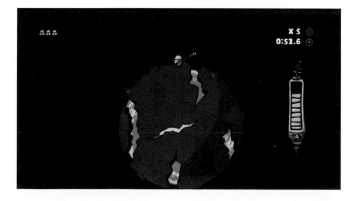

Figure 7.4. The area in red (the outer 15 percent of the screen) is outside of the safe frame.

Figure 7.5. Level selection screen in *aliEnd* [Pile 12].

7.5   Menus

Menus can be very platform specific. The way you interact with a menu via a mouse is significantly different than what you can do with a game pad. Additionally, when working with a touch device, you want to ensure that the interactive features are not too small and that important information is not obscured by the fingers of a player trying to interact with the system (see Figure 7.5).

Good menu design is an art; unfortunately, the details of that art are far beyond the scope of this text. However, as a graphics programmer, it will be your job to implement the system devised by the UI designer.

One useful tip when building your game menu is to ensure that you do not use a change in color to represent text that is selected from a list of choices. Even though this will work well when you have several orange items in a list and the one that is selected is green (as in Figure 7.6), if you instead have only two items in the list, it is impossible to tell if the selected item is the orange one or the green one (see Figure 7.7).

Instead, ensure that the selected item has something other than color to distinguish it. An easy solution is to have the selected item pulse. Thus, it is clear not only which item is currently the one that is selected (the pulsating one) but also that the screen is not static.

Figure 7.6. Using colors to highlight the player's selection works fine when there are many options.

Figure 7.7. Using colors to highlight the player's selection does not work when there are only two options.

Exercises: Challenges

Challenge 7.1. Implement a second language. Load the languages from a file and allow the user to swap between languages. (If you're not bilingual, use Google Translate or a similar tool to test localization within your game system. Of course you'll want to find a better solution before you ship your game.)

Challenge 7.2. Create and implement a function that will automatically wrap lines in a text string given a specific desired maximum display width.

Challenge 7.3. Expand on the implementation of Challenge 7.2 by adding a feature that will automatically scroll text when the text string exceeds a maximum screen height.

Part III

Advanced Graphics

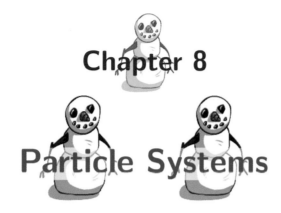

Chapter 8
Particle Systems

After animation, nothing brings a game world alive like particle effects (see, for example, Figure 8.1). Whether it's a crackling fire, a flurry of snow, or an explosion of debris, all these effects can be created with a *particle system*.

We have already seen one type of particle system. The tail of the dragon in Section 4.3.4 could be considered a set of *static* particles. That is, the segments of the tail act as independent particles but are attached to the main body. The particles exist as long as the main body exists.

The type of particles we look at in this chapter are sometimes called *animated particles* to distinguish them from static particles. Animated particles are often generated from a single point referred to as a *particle emitter*. These particles are generated from that given point in space, exist for a

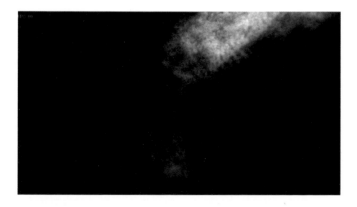

Figure 8.1. Fire and smoke particles, by Christopher Brough.

finite lifetime, and then fade out of existence. This chapter focuses on systems for generating this type of animated particle, but many of the same concepts could be applied to create a static particle system as well.

Both 2D and 3D games have many examples of particle systems. Examples of various particle effects can be viewed in Figures 8.17–8.19.

This chapter goes through the steps needed to build a robust particle effects system, starting with theory and ending with multiple examples of implementation. The chapter ends with a discussion of how to build the tools that will allow the programmer to hand the work of creating and editing the effects back to the artists.

The particle system is a hierarchical structure, starting with nothing more than a single sprite:

1. **Particle:** an individual *sprite* that can move independently.

2. **Particle effect:** a set of *particles* that, when combined, create a particular effect (such as fire).

3. **Particle system:** a library of *particle effects*, designed to work within your game or application.

To build a robust particle system capable of displaying a variety of particle effects, it is easiest to start by examining a single particle and then work your way up to the entire system.

8.1   What Is a Particle?

8.1.1   The Forest and the Trees

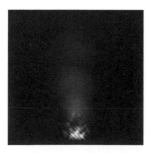

Figure 8.2. Fire and smoke particles, by Jacob Neville.

An individual particle is often short lived, fading into existence then fading back out moments later. The particle may accelerate as it is carried on the wind or it may float to the ground. A particle may be a lick of flame (Figure 8.2), a wisp of smoke, or a leaf falling from a tree.

What makes a particle uniquely different when compared to other game objects is that particles rarely have any effect on the game world. A fire may cause a player damage, perhaps by a comparison between the player's position with a radius around the source. However, the individual particles of flame are graphical only and should not affect the game play. For example, if a player is using a slower computer, the number of particles generated by the flame could be limited. The result might be a less impressive looking fire, but the effect of the fire should remain unchanged.

Similarly, particle positions should not need to be sent between players in a networked game. The two players may both have smoke particles that are generated from a smoldering building, but it is not important for the individual particles to exist in the same location on both PCs.

Let's start with some basic values we need in order to track the particle. This is in addition to the basic information we need for displaying the sprite itself, such as the texture and the sprite's location on that texture.

```
public int m_iAge;
```

This first value is the particle's lifespan in milliseconds. Once the particle's age is below zero, it should be considered to be dead. The initial age for a particle may be as much as a few seconds to as little as 500 milliseconds. Rain or smoke particles could exist even longer, whereas particles from fire and explosions would range on the shorter lifespans.

```
public Vector2 m_vPos;
public Vector2 m_vVel;
public Vector2 m_vAcc;

public float m_fDampening;
```

The first set of values above track the particle's position and how it might change over time. For example, a particle affected by gravity needs an acceleration value, and a particle emitted from an explosion might have a high initial velocity.

The fourth value in the list is used for wind resistance or other types of friction that decelerate the particle's velocity over time along an axis aligned with the current velocity. This should be a value between 0 and 1, such that 1.0 represents no friction at all.

Your particle class will need functions to create the new particle, as well as to update and draw it. Use the following code to get started, but the actual implementation is up to you. Notice that I have added a reference to a sprite class—that's something you need to create yourself.

```
public class cParticle
  {
    public int m_iAge;

    public Vector2 m_vPos;
    public Vector2 m_vVel;
    public Vector2 m_vAcc;

    public float m_fDampening;

    public cSprite   m_cSprite;

    public cParticle()
    {
```

```
15    m_cSprite = new cSprite();
    }

    public void Create(Texture2D texture, int ageInMS, Vector2
        pos, Vector2 vel, Vector2 acc, float damp)
    {
20      m_iAge = ageInMS;
      m_vPos = pos;
      m_vVel = vel;
      m_vAcc = acc;
      m_fDampening = damp;
25      m_cSprite.m_tTexture = texture;
    }

    public void UpdatePos(GameTime gameTime)
    {
30      m_vVel *= m_fDampening;
      m_vVel += (m_vAcc * (float)gameTime.ElapsedGameTime.
          TotalSeconds);
      m_vPos += (m_vVel * (float)gameTime.ElapsedGameTime.
          TotalSeconds);

      m_cSprite.m_vPos = m_vPos;
35    }

    public void Update(GameTime gameTime)
    {
      if (m_iAge < 0)
40        return;

      m_iAge -= gameTime.ElapsedGameTime.Milliseconds;

      UpdatePos(gameTime);
45    }

    public void Draw(SpriteBatch batch)
    {
      if (m_iAge < 0)
50        return;

      m_cSprite.Draw(batch);
    }
}
```

The Update function updates the particle age and then calls the function that updates the particle's velocity and position. As we cover the other parts of a particle, we add more functionality to the update.

In order to test the single particle, you can create a testing environment. Start with an XNA game shell and add the following:

```
1   cParticle myParticle;
    Texture2D spriteSheet;
```

```
    \\In Constructor:
 5  myParticle = new cParticle();

    \\In Load Content():
    spriteSheet = Content.Load<Texture2D>("whiteStar");

10  \\In Update():
    if (Keyboard.GetState().IsKeyDown(Keys.Up))
      {
        int initAge = 3000; //3 seconds
        Vector2 initPos = new Vector2(400, 400);
15      Vector2 initVel = new Vector2(0, -100);
        Vector2 initAcc = new Vector2(0, 75);
        float initDamp = 1.0f; //No friction
        myParticle.Create(spriteSheet, initAge, initPos, initVel,
            initAcc, initDamp);
      }
20
    myParticle.Update(gameTime);

    \\In Draw():
    spriteBatch.Begin(SpriteSortMode.FrontToBack, BlendState.
        NonPremultiplied);
25  myParticle.Draw(spriteBatch);
    spriteBatch.End();
```

In this example, the particle is created with an initial upward velocity; however, the downward acceleration eventually overcomes the upward velocity. After three seconds, the particle is considered dead and is no longer updated or drawn to the screen.

Now try modifying the initial values used to create the particle to see what kind of motion you can create.

8.1.2 Particle Rotation

This next set of values are used to track the rotation of the particle (Figure 8.3). It is unlikely that the particle will use rotational acceleration, but if needed, it could be added. A dampening value has been added for rotational friction.

```
 1  public float m_fRot;
    public float m_fRotVel;
    public float m_fRotDampening;
```

As with the position, you need to add initial values to the Create Particle function. I have listed below a possible Update function for the particle class.

Figure 8.3. Sample: particle rotation.

```
 1  public void UpdateRot(GameTime gameTime)
    {
      m_fRot *= m_fRotDampening;
```

```
         m_fRot  += (m_fRotVel  * (float)gameTime.ElapsedGameTime.
             TotalSeconds);
 5
         m_cSprite.m_fRotation = m_fRot;
     }

     public void Update(GameTime gameTime)
10   {
         if (m_iAge < 0)
             return;
         m_iAge  -= gameTime.ElapsedGameTime.Milliseconds;

15       UpdatePos(gameTime);
         UpdateRot(gameTime);
     }
```

8.1.3   Particle Scale

Just like position and rotation, it is likely that a particle's scale will change over time (Figure 8.4). Since it is graphically important that the scale of a sprite not exceed certain values, I have added a maximum scale. Alternatively, you could use an initial and final scale and linearly interpolate between the two scales based on the particle's age (as we will do with the particle's color). However, that would prevent the scale from growing and then shrinking.

```
 1   public float m_fScale;
     public float m_fScaleVel;
     public float m_fScaleAcc;
     public float m_fScaleMax;
```

Figure 8.4. Particles scale defined in code, by Christopher Brough.

Once again, I have provided a possible set of Update functions for your particle class. You need to set the initial values appropriately in your Create function.

```
 1   public void UpdateScale(GameTime gameTime)
     {
         m_fScaleVel += (m_fScaleAcc * (float)gameTime.
             ElapsedGameTime.TotalSeconds);
         m_fScale += (m_fScaleVel * (float)gameTime.ElapsedGameTime.
             TotalSeconds);
 5       m_fScale = MathHelper.Clamp(m_fScale, 0.0f, m_fScaleMax);

         m_cSprite.m_fScale = m_fScale;
     }

10   public void Update(GameTime gameTime)
     {
         if (m_iAge < 0)
```

```
    return;
    m_iAge  -= gameTime.ElapsedGameTime.Milliseconds;

    UpdatePos(gameTime);
    UpdateRot(gameTime);
    UpdateScale(gameTime);
}
```

In this case, we have clamped the scale to be between 0 and the maximum defined scale. An interesting set of initial values might be something like the following code sample.

```
int initAge = 3000; //3 seconds
Vector2 initPos = new Vector2(400, 400);
Vector2 initVel = new Vector2(0, -100);
Vector2 initAcc = new Vector2(0, 75);
float initDamp = 1.0f;

float initRot = 0.0f;
float initRotVel = 2.0f;
float initRotDamp = 0.99f;

float initScale = 0.2f;
float initScaleVel = 0.2f;
float initScaleAcc = -0.1f;
float maxScale = 1.0f;

myParticle.Create(initAge, initPos, initVel, initAcc,
    initDamp, initRot, initRotVel, initRotDamp, initScale,
    initScaleVel, initScaleAcc, maxScale);
```

It is possible that you might want the particle to pulse in scale. In that case, a more robust solution is required. That is the first challenge at the end of this chapter.

8.1.4 Particle Color

Since most particles are short lived, modifying the particle's color is a great way to allow the particle to simply fade out. However, it is likely that you will want the particle to be fully visible for most of its lifespan then fade out during the last n milliseconds. For that reason, I have added a fade age value. When the particle's age is less than the fade age, the color will be linearly interpolated between the initial color and the final color. (See Figure 8.5.)

```
public Color m_cColor;
public Color m_cInitColor;
public Color m_cFinalColor;

public int m_iFadeAge;
```

Figure 8.5. Particle color defined in code, by Alex Tardif.

For simply fading the particle out, the initial and final colors might be set to white but the alpha value transitions from 255 to 0 over the fade-out period. Alternatively, a lick of fire may transition from blue to red.

These color values can make a significant difference to the appearance of the particle. In the first examples, therefore, we use a sprite consisting of nothing but a single white shape. The sprite will be blended with the colors as appropriate.

At any given point, each component of color will be a blend of the initial color and the final color, determined by the age. For example, the amount is determined by

$$\text{red} = \left(\text{init red} \times \frac{\text{age}}{\text{start fading age}}\right) + \left(\text{final red} \times \left(1 - \frac{\text{age}}{\text{start fading age}}\right)\right)$$

In code, the Update function to apply that *linear interpolation* will look something like the following code sample.

```
public void UpdateColor(GameTime gameTime)
{
   if ((m_iAge > m_iFadeAge) && (m_iFadeAge != 0))
   {
      m_cColor = m_cInitColor;
   }
   else
   {
      float amtInit = (float)m_iAge / (float)m_iFadeAge;
      float amtFinal = 1.0f - amtInit;
```

```
        m_cColor.R = (byte)((amtInit * m_cInitColor.R) + (
            amtFinal * m_cFinalColor.R));
        m_cColor.G = (byte)((amtInit * m_cInitColor.G) + (
            amtFinal * m_cFinalColor.G));
        m_cColor.B = (byte)((amtInit * m_cInitColor.B) + (
            amtFinal * m_cFinalColor.B));
15      m_cColor.A = (byte)((amtInit * m_cInitColor.A) + (
            amtFinal * m_cFinalColor.A));
    }

    m_cSprite.m_cColor = m_cColor;
  }
20
  public void Update(GameTime gameTime)
  {
    if (m_iAge < 0)
        return;
25  m_iAge -= gameTime.ElapsedGameTime.Milliseconds;

    UpdatePos(gameTime);
    UpdateRot(gameTime);
    UpdateScale(gameTime);
30  UpdateColor(gameTime);
  }
```

If you want your particle to cycle through a series of colors, you could create a small array of colors with associated time stamps.

However, even if you don't create something that extravagant, its still important to use actual color values instead of creating a color velocity. This is because we want our artists to use our particle system to fine-tune the values. Creating a color velocity might make sense from a programmer's perspective, but it would add a layer of complexity that most artists would not appreciate.

Your job as a graphics programmer is to bridge the gap between the code and the art. This includes creating artist-friendly tools. The end goal should be the creation of a flexible particle system that can be given to the artists and designers without needing any further work from the programming team. You don't want to be asked to edit code every time the designer wants more flames or the artist wants the smoke to be a slightly different shade of blue.

8.2 Creating Effects

Now that we have a fairly robust particle class, we need to build a system that will generate and manage many particles at once. As a combined set, these particles will create the desired effect.

Consider a particle effect class with the following member variables.

```
public Texture2D particleTexture;

public Vector2 m_vOrigin;
public float m_fOriginRadius;

public int m_iEffectDuration;
public int m_iNewParticleAmount;
public int m_iBurstFrequencyMS;
public int m_iBurstCountdownMS;

public List<cParticle> m_lParticles;
```

The first value is obviously the texture. We may use different textures for different effects, but for now we'll just use this one.

The next two values (`Origin` and `OriginRadius`) designate a circular area from which the effect will be generated.

The third set of values controls the size and duration of the effect. `EffectDuration` designates how long the effect will generate particles; however, the effect should not be considered dead until all the particles within the effect are also dead.

`NewParticleAmount` indicates how many particles should be generated at each burst, and `BurstFrequency` indicates the length of time between bursts, which is tracked with the `BurstCountdown` variable. For example, if you want five particles every frame, you would set `NewParticleAmount` to 5 and `BurstFrequency` to 16 (60 frames per 1000 ms). If you wanted to generate only one new particle every second, you would set `NewParticleAmount` to 1 and set `BurstFrequency` to 1,000 ms.

Finally, the last member variable is the C# list containing all the particles. Let's start by generating one particle every frame for ten seconds. First we need to create a new particle list and initialize the effect, setting the duration, particle amount, and frequency. We also need to load the texture that will be used by the particle.

```
public cEffect()
{
  m_allParticles = new List<cParticle>();
}

public void Initialize()
{
  m_iEffectDuration = 10000;
  m_iNewParticleAmount = 1;
  m_iBurstFrequencyMS = 16;
  m_iBurstCountdownMS = m_iBurstFrequencyMS;
}

public void LoadContent(ContentManager content)
```

```
15  {
        particleTexture = content.Load<Texture2D>("whiteStar");
    }

    public void createParticle()
20  {
        //...
    }
```

The first part of the update checks to see whether the effect is still active. If it is and it is also time for the next burst of particles, we can create as many particles as specified by NewParticleAmount. We will get to the details of what happens in createParticle() in a moment.

```
1   public void Update(GameTime gameTime)
    {
      m_iEffectDuration -= gameTime.ElapsedGameTime.Milliseconds;
      m_iBurstCountdownMS -= gameTime.ElapsedGameTime.
          Milliseconds;
5
      if ((m_iBurstCountdownMS <= 0) && (m_iEffectDuration >= 0))
      {
        for (int i = 0; i < m_iNewParticleAmount; i++)
          createParticle();
        m_iBurstCountdownMS = m_iBurstFrequencyMS;
10    }

      //...
```

In the second half of the update function, we step through all the particles, updating them each individually. And then, while we're looping through them, we also remove any particles that have expired.

```
1     for (int i = m_allParticles.Count()-1; i>=0; i--)
      {
        m_allParticles[i].Update(gameTime);

5       if (m_allParticles[i].m_iAge <= 0)
          m_allParticles.RemoveAt(i);
      }
    }
```

Note that we are traversing the list backwards. This is to ensure that we don't break the loop logic by removing a particle in the wrong order.

Note that using a list in this way may create a variety of memory and performance issues. We discuss that problem later in this chapter.

For the Draw function we simply call the Particle Draw function for each particle in the list of particles.

```
1   public void Draw(SpriteBatch batch)
    {
```

```
    batch.Begin();
    foreach (cParticle p in m_allParticles)
    {
5       p.Draw(batch);
    }
    batch.End();
}
```

What we have avoided up until this point is the Create Particle function. With the various values we have created, this function involves a lot of variables and may seem a bit unwieldy, but it's actually fairly simplistic. We have a variety of values that need to be set for a specific effect, and that is exactly what we are doing here.

```
1   public void createParticle()
    {
        int initAge = 3000; //3 seconds

5       Vector2 initPos = m_vOrigin;
        Vector2 initVel = new Vector2(((float)(100.0f * Math.Cos(
            m_iEffectDuration))),
                                    ((float)(100.0f * Math.Sin(
                                        m_iEffectDuration))));

        Vector2 initAcc = new Vector2(0, 75);
10      float initDamp = 1.0f;

        float initRot = 0.0f;
        float initRotVel = 2.0f;
        float initRotDamp = 0.99f;
15
        float initScale = 0.2f;
        float initScaleVel = 0.2f;
        float initScaleAcc = -0.1f;
        float maxScale = 1.0f;
20
        Color initColor = Color.White;
        Color finalColor = Color.White;
        finalColor.A = 0;
        int fadeAge = initAge;
25
        cParticle tempParticle = new cParticle();
        tempParticle.Create(particleTexture, initAge, initPos,
            initVel, initAcc, initDamp, initRot, initRotVel,
            initRotDamp, initScale, initScaleVel, initScaleAcc,
            maxScale, initColor, finalColor, fadeAge);
        m_allParticles.Add(tempParticle);
    }
```

Here, I set the variables and then create a temporary particle that I add to the particle list. The only slightly unusual aspect of this function is the use of the sine and cosine functions.

What I want to do is create a particle effect that emits particles with an initial velocity of 100, but I want the direction of that velocity to rotate as a function of time.

In this case, I know that `EffectDuration` counts down until it reaches zero. Using basic trigonometry, I know that I can set the components as follows, using the remaining time as the rotation amount. This works well because rotation values repeat after 2π:

$$x \text{ component} = 100 \times \cos(\text{remaining time}),$$
$$y \text{ component} = 100 \times \sin(\text{remaining time}).$$

The result is a spiraling particle emitter. As before, the particles fade from white to white with alpha set to zero, starting with an initial upward velocity and finally being turned around by the downward acceleration. Similarly, the individual particles start with an initial scale that begins by increasing but is eventually overwhelmed by the negative scale acceleration. The rotation of the individual particles is dampened with a value of 0.99, causing a resistance to the rotation over time.

Of course, for any of this to occur, we need to activate the particle effect within the main game.

Using an XNA game shell, we need only to add the following code:

```
//Member variables:
//...
cEffect myEffect;

//In Constructor:
myEffect = new cEffect();

//In Load Content:
//...
cEffect.LoadContent(Content);

//In Update:
//...

if (Keyboard.GetState().IsKeyDown(Keys.Up))
{
   myEffect.Initialize();
}

myEffect.Update(gameTime);
//...

//In Draw:
//...
myEffect.Draw(gameTime, spriteBatch);
//...
```

The result should look similar to Figure 8.6.

Figure 8.6. Example: particle spiral.

8.3   Blending Types

A discerning reader may have noticed a different value for the blending option in the previous example's Sprite Batch Begin function. That is, I used the value `BlendState.NonPremultiplied` instead of `BlendState.AlphaBlend`.

When blending a pixel with the pixel previously drawn to the back buffer, a calculation must be made to determine the resultant color. It's not enough to simply add the individual RGBA values together because the result value would likely result in a number higher than a byte (255).

In XNA, we are given four options for *blending*:

1. **Additive:** With additive blending, the alpha value is ignored but the colors are still blended. This means that when dark red is blended with more dark red, the result is a higher value of red and thus a lighter red.

2. **AlphaBlend:** With alpha blending, the source and destination colors are blended by using the alpha value. The result of this may be a bit unexpected. Given our knowledge of color, the assumption might be that if you set the alpha value to zero, the sprite would be completely transparent. But that's not quite the case, and the reason is a bit

beyond the scope of this book. The important thing to know is that if you want to set the alpha value of a color when using AlphaBlend, instead of manually setting the alpha value, simply multiply the entire color by the desired alpha value.

3. **Non-premultiplied:** By default, XNA will premultiply the alpha values of your sprites as part of the content pipeline. If you do not want this to occur, set `Premultiply Alpha` to `False` in the property value of the texture. I have included a link on the companion website, http://www.2dGraphicsProgramming.com, for more information about premultiplied alphas. This allows us to get the result we would have otherwise expected by setting the alpha value to zero as described above for AlphaBlend mode.

4. **Opaque:** The simplest blending is no blending. Opaque simply overwrites the color with the new color.

The variation of results from choosing a particular blending mode are significant, especially when working with multiple layers of particles in an attempt to create various effects.

In Figures 8.7–8.9, the particles start with a value of dark red (R: 139; G: 0; B: 0; A: 255) and transition to a value of dark red without alpha. The clear color is blue to show the way the background color affects the blended results. In parts (a), I have set the alpha value manually (R: 139; G: 0; B: 0; A: 0). In parts (b), I have used the built-in XNA operator override of multiplying a color by an alpha value.

As you can see, the differences are significant. I have not included opaque blending because it is rarely useful. You can try it for yourself to see the result.

Note both the way the final color blends with the background blue as well as the way the sprite blends with other sprites. The only two that match are the Figures 8.8(b) and 8.9(a). This has to do with the equations used to blend source and destination colors.

We can use this variety to our advantage when creating various effects. For this reason, I have added another Member variable to the effect class.

```
//Effect member variable
public BlendState    m_eBlendType;

//Effect Draw
batch.Begin(SpriteSortMode.BackToFront, m_eBlendType);
//...
```

Figure 8.7. Additive with (a) `finalColor.A = 0` and (b) `finalColor = finalColor * 0`.

Figure 8.8. AlphaBlend with (a) `finalColor.A = 0` and (b) `finalColor = finalColor * 0`.

Figure 8.9. Non-premultiplied with (a) `finalColor.A = 0` and (b) `finalColor = finalColor * 0`.

8.4 Types of Effects

Now that we have a simple effect system, let us take a moment to look at how our various starting parameters might be used to generate specific effects. In each of these, we will modify the Create Particle function and initialization values.

8.4.1 Fire

For a simple fire effect (Figure 8.10), I start with randomly generating ten particles around a particular point in every frame. If the particles are generated at the left of the origin, they are given an initial velocity to the right. If they are generated at the right, they are given an initial velocity to the left. In addition, the particles have an upward velocity and random upward acceleration.

The particles blend from red (A = 255) to yellow (A = 0) by using additive blending, starting small and slowly scaling down the white circle texture.

Figure 8.10. Example: fire effect.

```
1   public void Initialize()
    {
      m_iEffectDuration = 60000;
      m_iNewParticleAmount = 10;
5     m_iBurstFrequencyMS = 16;
      m_iBurstCountdownMS = m_iBurstFrequencyMS;

      m_vOrigin = new Vector2(400, 400);
      m_iRadius = 50;
10    m_eBlendType = BlendState.Additive;
    }

    public void LoadContent(ContentManager content)
    {
15    particleTexture = content.Load<Texture2D>("whiteCircle");
    }

    public void createFireParticle()
    {
20    int initAge = 3000; //3 seconds
      int fadeAge = 2750;

      Vector2 initPos = m_vOrigin;
      Vector2 offset;
25    offset.X = ((float)(myRandom.Next(m_iRadius) * Math.Cos(
          myRandom.Next(360))));
      offset.Y = ((float)(myRandom.Next(m_iRadius) * Math.Sin(
          myRandom.Next(360))));
```

```
           initPos += offset;

           Vector2 initVel = Vector2.Zero;
30         initVel.X = -(offset.X * 0.5f);
           initVel.Y = 0.0f;

           Vector2 initAcc = new Vector2(0, -myRandom.Next(200));

35         float initDamp = 0.96f;

           float initRot = 0.0f;
           float initRotVel = 0.0f;
           float initRotDamp = 1.0f;
40
           float initScale = 0.5f;
           float initScaleVel = -0.1f;
           float initScaleAcc = 0.0f;
           float maxScale = 1.0f;
45
           Color initColor = Color.Red;
           Color finalColor = Color.Yellow;
           finalColor.A = 0;

50
           cParticle tempParticle = new cParticle();
           tempParticle.Create(particleTexture, initAge, initPos,
               initVel, initAcc, initDamp, initRot, initRotVel,
               initRotDamp, initScale, initScaleVel, initScaleAcc,
               maxScale, initColor, finalColor, fadeAge);
           m_allParticles.Add(tempParticle);
       }
```

We can create a wider flame base (Figure 8.11) by moving the origin along the x-axis while also increasing the number of particles that are generated in each frame.

Figure 8.11. Row of flames.

```
1   //In Initialization:
    m_vOrigin = new Vector2(640, 400);
    m_iNewParticleAmount = 50;

5   //In Create Particle, add:
    Vector2 offset2 = Vector2.Zero;
    offset2.X += (float)(400 * Math.Cos(m_iEffectDuration));
    initPos += offset2;
```

Then, with a few more modifications, we can create a faster blue-colored flame (Figure 8.12) that moves back and forth by modifying the values as in the following code:

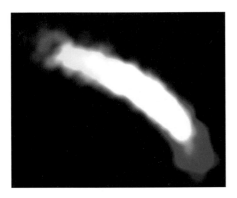

Figure 8.12. Moving blue flame.

Figure 8.13. Example: smoke effect.

```
1  //In Initialization:
   m_iNewParticleAmount = 15;
   m_iRadius = 30;

5  //In Create Particle:

   //Modify age of particles
   int initAge = 500 + (int)myRandom.Next(500); //3 seconds
   int fadeAge = initAge - (int)myRandom.Next(100);
10 //...

   //Decrease offset movement speed
   offset2.X += (float)(200 * Math.Cos(m_iEffectDuration/500.0f));
   //...
15
   //Increase y Velocity
   initVel.Y = -500;
   //...

20 //Modify y Acceleration
   Vector2 initAcc = new Vector2(0, -myRandom.Next(300));
   //...

   //Modify Color Range
25 Color initColor = Color.DarkBlue;
   Color finalColor = Color.DarkOrange;
```

8.4.2 Smoke

For smoke (Figure 8.13), I apply a process similar to that for the fire by using the white circle textures but with a more subtle effect. The color transitions from black (A = 128) to a dark gray defined by the RGBA values (R: 32; G: 32; B: 32; A: 0). Because the particles themselves are

almost completely transparent, the primary source of the effect occurs as
an interaction between the additive interaction of the blended particles:

```
public void Initialize()
{
    //Smoke
    m_iEffectDuration = 60000;
    m_iNewParticleAmount = 4;
    m_iBurstFrequencyMS = 16;
    m_iBurstCountdownMS = m_iBurstFrequencyMS;

    m_vOrigin = new Vector2(640, 640);
    m_iRadius = 50;
    m_eBlendType = BlendState.Additive;
}

public void createSmokeParticle()
{
    int initAge = 5000 + (int)myRandom.Next(5000);
    int fadeAge = initAge - (int)myRandom.Next(5000);

    Vector2 initPos = m_vOrigin;
    Vector2 offset;
    offset.X = ((float)(myRandom.Next(m_iRadius) * Math.Cos(
        myRandom.Next(360))));
    offset.Y = ((float)(myRandom.Next(m_iRadius) * Math.Sin(
        myRandom.Next(360))));
    initPos += offset;

    Vector2 offset2 = Vector2.Zero;
    offset2.X += (float)(400 * Math.Cos(m_iEffectDuration /
        500.0f));
    initPos += offset2;

    Vector2 initVel = Vector2.Zero;
    initVel.X = 0;//
    initVel.Y = -30 - myRandom.Next(30);

    Vector2 initAcc = new Vector2(10 + myRandom.Next(10), 0);

    float initDamp = 1.0f;

    float initRot = 0.0f;
    float initRotVel = 0.0f;
    float initRotDamp = 1.0f;

    float initScale = 0.6f;
    float initScaleVel = ((float)myRandom.Next(10))/50.0f;
    float initScaleAcc = 0.0f;
    float maxScale = 3.0f;

    Color initColor = Color.Black;
    initColor.A = 128;
```

```
      Color finalColor = new Color(32, 32, 32);
      finalColor.A = 0;

50    //Create and add particle to list as before
      //...

  }
```

In addition to generating smoke, a similar set of values could be used to generate fog, clouds, or mist. An even better result could be obtained by using a different texture, perhaps something that looked more like a puff of smoke. We could then randomly rotate the texture, creating more realistic-looking smoke.

8.4.3 Explosions

For an explosion (Figure 8.14), I generate many star particles in one frame. The particles are given high initial velocities and a downward acceleration. They are also given an acceleration value based on whether they are on the right or left side of the explosion base, as shown in the code below.

Figure 8.14. Example: explosion effect.

```
public void Initialize()
{
  //Explosion
  m_iEffectDuration = 16;
  m_iNewParticleAmount = 800;
  m_iBurstFrequencyMS = 16;
  m_iBurstCountdownMS = m_iBurstFrequencyMS;

  m_vOrigin = new Vector2(200, 720);
  m_iRadius = 20;
  m_eBlendType = BlendState.NonPremultiplied;
}

public void createExplosionParticle()
{
  int initAge = 3000 + (int)myRandom.Next(5000);
  int fadeAge = initAge /2;

  Vector2 initPos = m_vOrigin;
  Vector2 offset;
  offset.X = ((float)(myRandom.Next(m_iRadius) * Math.Cos(
      myRandom.Next(360))));
  offset.Y = ((float)(myRandom.Next(m_iRadius) * Math.Sin(
      myRandom.Next(360))));
  initPos += offset;

  Vector2 initVel = Vector2.Zero;
  initVel.X = myRandom.Next(500) + (offset.X * 30);
  initVel.Y = -60 * Math.Abs(offset.Y);

  Vector2 initAcc = new Vector2(0, 400);

  float initDamp = 1.0f;

  float initRot = 0.0f;
  float initRotVel = initVel.X / 50.0f;
  float initRotDamp = 0.97f;

  float initScale = 0.1f + ((float)myRandom.Next(10)) / 50.0f
      ;
  float initScaleVel = ((float)myRandom.Next(10)-5) / 50.0f;
  float initScaleAcc = 0.0f;
  float maxScale = 1.0f;

  byte randomGray = (byte)(myRandom.Next(128) + 128);
  Color initColor = new Color(randomGray, 0, 0);

  Color finalColor = new Color(32, 32, 32);
  finalColor = Color.Black;

  //Create and add particle to list as before
  //...
}
```

This effect could be used for a variety of types of explosions, from meteor impacts to fireworks. This is also a great effect for smaller-scale events, such as when a child jumps into a pile of leaves. In fact, a similar type of explosion of feathers happens in *Flock!* [Proper Games 09] every time a chicken lands on the ground.

8.4.4 Snow or Rain

In this example, I have created a simple falling snowflake effect (Figure 8.15) by using a snowflake texture. I first calculate a particle scale, and then I modify the particle age and fall velocity based on the scale so that smaller flakes fall slower and last longer, creating a very simplistic parallax effect.

I've also changed the clear color to something slightly more appropriate for this example.

Figure 8.15. Example: snowflake effect.

```
1   public void SnowInitialize()
    {
      //Snow
      m_iEffectDuration = 60000;
5     m_iNewParticleAmount = 1;
      m_iBurstFrequencyMS = 64;
      m_iBurstCountdownMS = m_iBurstFrequencyMS;

      m_vOrigin = new Vector2(640, -50);
10    m_iRadius = 50;
      m_eBlendType = BlendState.NonPremultiplied;
    }

    public void createSnowParticle()
15  {
      float initScale = 0.1f + ((float)myRandom.Next(10)) / 20.0f
          ;
      float initScaleVel = 0.0f;
      float initScaleAcc = 0.0f;
      float maxScale = 1.0f;

20
      int initAge = (int)(10000/initScale);
      int fadeAge = initAge;

      Vector2 initPos = m_vOrigin;
25    Vector2 offset;
      offset.X = ((float)(myRandom.Next(m_iRadius) * Math.Cos(
          myRandom.Next(360))));
      offset.Y = ((float)(myRandom.Next(m_iRadius) * Math.Sin(
          myRandom.Next(360))));
      initPos += offset;
```

```
30    Vector2 offset2 = Vector2.Zero;
      offset2.X += (float)(600 * Math.Cos(m_iEffectDuration
          /500.0));
      initPos += offset2;


35    Vector2 initVel = Vector2.Zero;
      initVel.X = myRandom.Next(10) - 5;
      initVel.Y = 100 * initScale;

      Vector2 initAcc = new Vector2(0, 0);
40
      float initDamp = 1.0f;

      float initRot = 0.0f;
      float initRotVel = initVel.X / 5.0f; ;
45    float initRotDamp = 1.0f;

      Color initColor = Color.White;
      Color finalColor = Color.White;
      finalColor.A = 0;
50
      //Create and add particle to list as before
      //...
  }
```

The use of the snowflake sprite creates a really nice effect. An enhancement to this example would be to add some variety in the snowflakes, editing the code to select randomly from a set of snowflake textures.

8.4.5   Other Effects

Figure 8.16. Example: silly effect of head on fire.

We have seen how particles can be emitted from points and by lines when we offset the origin. But what if we were to update the effect origin through our game code? We would then have the ability, for example, to create effects like flames shooting out from the top of a character's head (Figure 8.16). We can achieve a variety of other effects with particles that might not seem as obvious as the examples we have looked at so far.

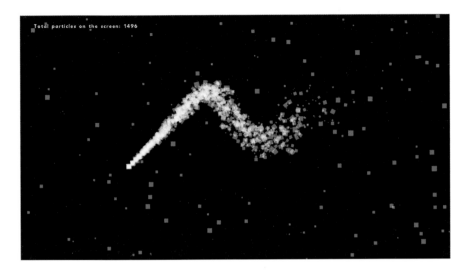

Figure 8.17. Various particles, by Brett Chalupa.

Consider what would happen if we set the effect origin to match the player's feet and generated a new particle whenever the player was moving. This would allow us to create footsteps in dirt or tire tracks through snow.

Another option is to use the player's current sprite as the particle. By leaving behind a series of particles in the shape of the player as the sprite moved, we could create a 1970s blurred running effect.

From an explosion of sparkles as a player receives a gold medal award to the mud thrown from motorcycle tire, the variety of possible effects that we can create with particles is limited only by our imagination. A few further examples of various effects in action can be seen in Figures 8.17, 8.18, and 8.19.

8.4.6 Combining Types

Now that we have looked at some of the effects that are possible with particle systems, it is time to make the system a bit more robust. The first thing we need to do is to define the various types of effects that are possible to generate.

We start by creating an enumerated type and adding an instance of that type to the effect class, as shown in the following code.

```
public enum eEffectType
{
  smoke,
  fire,
  explosion,
```

Figure 8.18. Particles create smoke trails and explosions, by Alex Toulan.

```
      snow
   }

   public class cEffect
   {
      public eEffectType m_eType;

      public Texture2D particleTexture;
      static Texture2D snowflakeTexture;
      static Texture2D circleTexture;
      static Texture2D starTexture;

      //...

      static public void LoadContent(ContentManager content)
      {
         snowflakeTexture = content.Load<Texture2D>("snowFlake");
         circleTexture = content.Load<Texture2D>("whiteCircle");
         starTexture = content.Load<Texture2D>("whiteStar");
      }
```

Notice that the individual textures and the LoadContent function are now listed as static to ensure that the textures are loaded only once during the load content phase and are independent of the individual instances of the effect class.

We have already created the functions to initialize and create the particles. Now we just need to ensure they are utilized as defined by the enumerated effect type we just added.

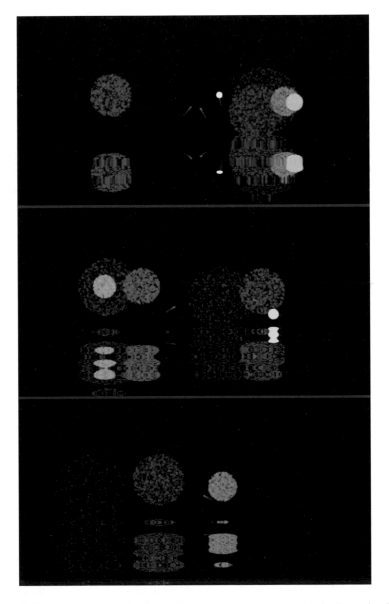

Figure 8.19. Particles create fireworks over rippling water, by Andrew Auclair.

```
1   public void Initialize(eEffectType pType)
    {
      m_eType = pType;

5     switch (m_eType)
      {
        case eEffectType.fire:
          FireInitialize();
          break;
10      case eEffectType.smoke:
          SmokeInitialize();
          break;
        case eEffectType.explosion:
          ExplosionInitialize();
15        break;
        case eEffectType.snow:
          SnowInitialize();
          break;
      }
20  }

    public void createParticle()
    {
      switch (m_eType)
25    {
        case eEffectType.fire:
          createFireParticle();
          break;
        case eEffectType.smoke:
30        createSmokeParticle();
          break;
        case eEffectType.explosion:
          createExplosionParticle();
          break;
35      case eEffectType.snow:
          createSnowParticle();
          break;
      }
    }
40
    public void SnowInitialize()
    {
      //Explosion
      particleTexture = snowflakeTexture;
45    //...
    }

    public void FireInitialize()
    {
50    //Fire
      particleTexture = circleTexture;
      //...
    }
```

```
55  public void SmokeInitialize()
    {
      //Smoke
      particleTexture = circleTexture;
      //...
    }
60  public void ExplosionInitialize()
    {
      //Explosion
      particleTexture = starTexture;
      //...
65  }
```

In our main game, we can now initialize a specific type of particle effect at the press of a button.

```
1   if (Keyboard.GetState().IsKeyDown(Keys.Up))
    {
      myEffect.Initialize(eEffectType.explosion);
    }
5   if (Keyboard.GetState().IsKeyDown(Keys.Down))
    {
      myEffect.Initialize(eEffectType.fire);
    }
    if (Keyboard.GetState().IsKeyDown(Keys.Left))
10  {
      myEffect.Initialize(eEffectType.snow);
    }
    if (Keyboard.GetState().IsKeyDown(Keys.Right))
    {
15    myEffect.Initialize(eEffectType.smoke);
    }
```

This is certainly something fun to play with, but we are not yet done. Since every time a key is pressed, the same effect is reinitialized, a better solution would be to create a new effect and not reuse the same one.

Before we can do that, though, we need to add one more function: when we build the effect system, we need to know when a particular effect is completely dead. As mentioned before, the effect duration tells us only how long the effect is generating new particles, not whether those particles are still alive.

For our current particle list, however, the solution is simple enough:

```
1   public bool isAlive()
    {
      if (m_iEffectDuration > 0)
        return true;
5     if (m_allParticles.Count() > 0)
        return true;
      return false;
    }
```

8.5   An Effect System

We now have all we need to build an *effect system*. This is the third and final tier, as we have moved from particle, to effect, to effect system.

The effect system can be thought of as a software engineering structure for managing all the effects. Listed below is the entirety of a simple effect manager.

```
1  public class cEffectManager
   {
     public List<cEffect> m_lAllEffects;

5    public cEffectManager()
     {
       m_lAllEffects = new List<cEffect>();
     }

10   public void LoadContent(ContentManager Content)
     {
       cEffect.LoadContent(Content);
     }

15   public void AddEffect(eEffectType type)
     {
       cEffect tempEffect = new cEffect();
       tempEffect.Initialize(type);
       m_lAllEffects.Add(tempEffect);
20   }

     public void Update(GameTime gameTime)
     {
       for (int i = m_lAllEffects.Count() - 1; i >= 0; i--)
25     {
         m_lAllEffects[i].Update(gameTime);

         if (!m_lAllEffects[i].isAlive())
           m_lAllEffects.RemoveAt(i);
30     }
     }

     public void Draw(SpriteBatch batch)
     {
35     foreach (cEffect e in m_lAllEffects)
       {
         e.Draw(batch);
       }
     }
40 }
```

Just like the effect class stores a list of particles, the effect manager stores a list of effects. The effect manager allows us to create a new effect through an AddEffect function.

In the main game loop, the code might look something like the following:

```
public class Game1 : Microsoft.Xna.Framework.Game
{
  GraphicsDeviceManager graphics;
  SpriteBatch spriteBatch;

  cEffectManager myEffectsManager;
  int keyboardDelayCounter = 0;
  int keyboardDelay = 300;

  public Game1()
  {
    graphics = new GraphicsDeviceManager(this);
    Content.RootDirectory = "Content";

    myEffectsManager = new cEffectManager();
  }

  protected override void Initialize()
  {
    graphics.PreferredBackBufferWidth = 1280;
    graphics.PreferredBackBufferHeight = 720;
    graphics.ApplyChanges();

    base.Initialize();
  }

  protected override void LoadContent()
  {
    spriteBatch = new SpriteBatch(GraphicsDevice);
    myEffectsManager.LoadContent(Content);
  }

  protected override void Update(GameTime gameTime)
  {
    if (Keyboard.GetState().IsKeyDown(Keys.Escape))
      this.Exit();

    if (keyboardDelayCounter > 0)
    {
      keyboardDelayCounter -= gameTime.ElapsedGameTime.
        Milliseconds;
    }
    else
    {
      if (Keyboard.GetState().IsKeyDown(Keys.Up))
      {
          myEffectsManager.AddEffect(eEffectType.explosion);
          keyboardDelayCounter = keyboardDelay;
      }
      if (Keyboard.GetState().IsKeyDown(Keys.Down))
      {
          myEffectsManager.AddEffect(eEffectType.fire);
```

```
              keyboardDelayCounter = keyboardDelay;
        }
        //...

55
        }

    myEffectsManager.Update(gameTime);

60  base.Update(gameTime);
    }

    protected override void Draw(GameTime gameTime)
    {
65      Color clearColor = Color.Black;
        GraphicsDevice.Clear(clearColor);

        myEffectsManager.Draw(spriteBatch);

70      base.Draw(gameTime);
    }
}
```

After implementation and a little testing of the above code, you should notice a very significant problem. Even on a very fast computer, once we have a large number of particles moving around the scene, the processing requirements are too much for the system to handle. In the next section, we work through the options for improving the performance of the particle system.

8.6 Optimization

8.6.1 Limitations

The first and easiest optimization is to simply place a limit on the number of particles that can exist within a given particle effect and then a limit on the total number of particles being processed by all currently active effects.

We need to approach this problem on two fronts. First, we need to ensure that new particles are not created when the maximum number of particles has been reached. But more important, we need to ensure good communication with our artists and designers on these limits. The tools we build to help them create effects should help with this as well.

To set your particle cap, you first need to understand what is causing the drop in frame rate. The number of particles your particle system can process can be limited by the simulation stage (processing orientation and position updates) or the rendering phase (drawing the particles to the screen). Both cases have nested for loops (processing every particle for every effect). It is important to understand your platform to understand where the bottleneck is occurring.

An easy solution is to simply cap the number of particles available for a given effect by adding an if statement that will not create new particles when the cap has been reached. However, we also need to consider the number of effects we have at any given time. After all, one effect with 10,000 active particles will likely have computational and rendering requirements very similar to ten effects each rendered with 1,000 particles.

Additionally, tracking the current total number of particles on the screen can be useful for debugging purposes. In so doing, you may find that you need different particle limits for various platforms; for example, a PC may be able to handle significantly more particles than a mobile phone. You want to design a solution that ensures you get a good effect on all systems to which you plan to deploy.

8.6.2   Early Particle Removal

In some cases (e.g., explosive effects), you may still be processing particles long after they have left the field of view. You may find improved performance by marking as dead the particles that have left the screen. If you do that, however, you must use care. If you have a moving camera, a particle that was once off-screen may need to be visible once again when the camera moves.

8.6.3   Memory Management and Particle Reuse

Although doing your best to limit the total number of particles may help to improve performance, it might be addressing the symptom rather than the underlying problem. For example, your game may start to drop in frame rate when 5,000 particles are being generated, but another game may run 30,000 particles on the same platform without any difficulty.

In the first particle example in Section 8.2, we used the C# List< T > data structure to store our array of particles. Let's consider, however, what is happening within the memory of a list. The items in the list are quickly created and removed, and each of these list operations has its own overhead set. As an item in a list is removed, the memory making up that list is resized.

As a first step, if you want to increase performance, you can make a decision never to remove a particle from a list. Instead, you could start with a specific number of items in the list and skip both processing and rendering any dead particle. When it's time to create a new particle, you would simply find the first dead particle and reset it with the new values.

A better solution may be found through using a data structure with less overhead. Consider using a fixed size array instead of the list. You may also find success by using LINQ for processing the elements within the particle list. No matter what the case, you want to employ good benchmarking and timing techniques so you know what works best for your specific system. Some compilers are very good at optimizing, so you want to be sure that your "solution" really is faster than the built-in functionality.

Of course, these same techniques could be applied to the list of particle effects. It is reasonable at initialization to consider a solution that defines the memory necessary for all the particles that will ever be used in the game. In such a case, there will be very little worry about unexpected consequences of high particle count at some later point in the game.

8.6.4 Multithreading

Another great option for improving the performance of your particle system is to consider the fact that the particle system may be running completely independently of other game events. Particles are often generated, but they may never interact with other game data. As a result, they can be a perfect option for *multithreading*. Depending on your system, this may offer significant improvements on your game performance.

However, be aware that some systems have better multithreading options than others. You may decide you want to limit the number of particles based on the availability of multiple processors.

Exercises: Challenges

Challenge 8.1. Alter the particle system to allow for particles that pulse in size.

Challenge 8.2. Create a fireworks particle effect, as in Figure 8.19.

Challenge 8.3. Add the ability to use animated sprites and create an effect that makes use of the animated sprites. This would be ideal for a kaleidoscope of butterflies.

Challenge 8.4. Add the ability to cycle through a range of colors. Create an effect that makes use of this feature.

Challenge 8.5. Build an effect editor into your system. Artists should be able to test the results.

Challenge 8.6. Add the ability to count the total number of particles currently being rendered. Use this counter to limit the creation of new particles.

Challenge 8.7. Convert the particle system to use an array instead of `List<T>`. Analyze any performance differences.

Challenge 8.8. Convert your particle system to run on a separate thread.

Chapter 9

GPU Programming

9.1 Pixel Modification

So far we have manipulated the scale, orientation, and color of sprites to create various effects in our game. As we have seen, this allows for a great deal of creativity. But what happens if we want to modify individual pixels, as required to create the blur effect seen in Figure 9.1?

Consider the following code, in which we generate a gradient mixture of blue and red. We first create a 2D array of colors, and then we create a texture using that color array.

```
protected override void LoadContent()
{
  int width = 256;
  int height = 256;

  //Create 2D array of colors
  Color[] arrayOfColor = new Color[width * height];

  for (int j = 0; j < height; j++)
    for (int i = 0; i < width; i++)
    {
        arrayOfColor[i + (width * j)] = new Color(i, 0, j);
    }

  //Place color array into a texture
  pixelsTexture = new Texture2D(GraphicsDevice, width, height
    );
  pixelsTexture.SetData<Color>(arrayOfColor);
}
```

Once the new texture has been created, we can now add that into our Draw function:

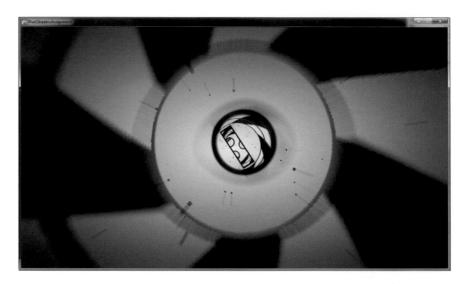

Figure 9.1. Blur effect by Adam Reed in his unpublished game, *Tunnel Vision*.

```
spriteBatch.Begin();
spriteBatch.Draw(pixelsTexture, Vector2.Zero, Color.White);
spriteBatch.End();
```

The result of drawing this new texture to the screen can be seen in Figure 9.2.

This is easy enough, and we could take this one step further. Instead of creating a new color array, we could get the color array from an existing texture. We could then modify that array in an interesting way and create a second texture with our modified color array.

For example, in the following code I have inverted the color data for the snowman.

```
protected override void LoadContent()
{

    spriteBatch = new SpriteBatch(GraphicsDevice);

    int width = 256;
    int height = 256;
    spriteSheet = Content.Load<Texture2D>("snow_assets");

    //Get 2D array of colors from sprite sheet
    Color[] arrayOfColor = new Color[width * height];
    spriteSheet.GetData<Color>(0, new Rectangle(0,128, 256,
        256), arrayOfColor, 0, (width * height));
```

Figure 9.2. Gradient created from a color array.

Figure 9.3. Snowman and inverted snowman.

```
     //Place color array into a texture
15   pixelsTexture1 = new Texture2D(GraphicsDevice, width,
         height);
     pixelsTexture1.SetData<Color>(arrayOfColor);

     for (int j = 0; j < height; j++)
       for (int i = 0; i < width; i++)
20     {
         int currentElement = i + (width * j);
         arrayOfColor[currentElement].R = (byte)(255 -
             arrayOfColor[currentElement].R);
         arrayOfColor[currentElement].G = (byte)(255 -
             arrayOfColor[currentElement].G);
         arrayOfColor[currentElement].B = (byte)(255 -
             arrayOfColor[currentElement].B);
25     }

     //Place color array into a texture
     pixelsTexture2 = new Texture2D(GraphicsDevice, width,
         height);
     pixelsTexture2.SetData<Color>(arrayOfColor);
30   }
```

Then in the following code, we draw the two newly created textures side by side. Note that we need to use the non-premultiplied blend state because we want to render based on the original unmodified alpha value.

```
1    spriteBatch.Begin(SpriteSortMode.BackToFront, BlendState.
         NonPremultiplied);
     spriteBatch.Draw(pixelsTexture1, Vector2.Zero, Color.White)
         ;
     spriteBatch.Draw(pixelsTexture2, new Vector2(256,0), Color.
         White);
     spriteBatch.End();
```

The result can be seen in Figure 9.3.

The ability to modify individual pixels provides a great deal of power to our graphics programming skills. Unfortunately, we will quickly run into limitations on what types of effects we can create based on the capabuility of the computer's CPU.

In the previous examples, we modified the graphics data as part of the LoadContent function. But what if we wanted to do something more dynamic, such as modifying the graphics data during the Update function. Let's consider the following addition to the previous code.

```
Vector2 pos = Vector2.Zero;
Vector2 vel = new Vector2(1.0f, 1.5f);

//...

public void updatePosition()
{
  pos += vel;

  if ((pos.X < 0) || (pos.X > 255))
    vel.X *= -1f;
  MathHelper.Clamp(pos.X, 0, 255);

  if ((pos.Y < 0) || (pos.Y > 255))
    vel.Y *= -1f;
  MathHelper.Clamp(pos.Y, 0, 255);
}

public void modifyPixelTextures2()
{
  int width = 256;
  int height = 256;

  //Get 2D array of colors from texture2
  Color[] arrayOfColor = new Color[width * height];
  pixelsTexture1.GetData<Color>(arrayOfColor);

  //Modify color array into a texture
  for (int j = 0; j < height; j++)
    for (int i = 0; i < width; i++)
    {
      int currElement = i + (scr_width * j);
      double distance = Math.Sqrt(Math.Pow(i-pos.X, 2) + Math
        .Pow(j-pos.Y, 2));
      double radius = 50;
      if (distance < radius)
      {
        arrayOfColor[currentElement].R = (byte)(255 -
          arrayOfColor[currentElement].R);
        arrayOfColor[currentElement].G = (byte)(255 -
          arrayOfColor[currentElement].G);
        arrayOfColor[currentElement].B = (byte)(255 -
          arrayOfColor[currentElement].B);
        arrayOfColor[currentElement].A = 255;
```

```
        }
      }

    //Place color array into a texture
45  pixelsTexture2.SetData<Color>(arrayOfColor);
    }

    protected override void Update(GameTime gameTime)
    {
50    //...
      updatePosition();
      modifyPixelTextures2();

      base.Update(gameTime);
55  }
```

With the addition of the above code, the inversion of the texture occurs dynamically around a given point that bounces around the screen (see Figure 9.4).

The distance formula is used here, which causes a square root function that can be computationally expensive to execute. As with any large loop that we need to process, this can be time consuming for the processor. And this is not just a one-time requirement—the loop must be processed for every frame. In this example, let's assume it requires eight CPU operations to calculate the square root; the result is that the CPU needs to perform more than 31 million operations per second just to create a dynamic inverted circle on a 256-square texture:

Figure 9.4. Snowman and inverted radius of snowman.

$$256 \times 256 \times 8 \ \frac{\text{operations}}{\text{calculation}} \times 60 \ \frac{\text{frames}}{\text{second}} = 31{,}457{,}280 \ \frac{\text{operations}}{\text{second}}.$$

Depending on the processor, this may be enough to slow down the frame rate. Even if not, it will add up quickly as we attempt to do more complicated effects across larger areas of the screen.

Note, however, that calculating the square root is overkill. When calculating distance, instead of comparing the square root to the radius, we can calculate the square of the radius by using the square of the distance. This simple modification (shown in the following code) ensures that we never need to perform the square root calculation when calculating distance.

```
1  double distanceSQR = Math.Pow(i-pos.X, 2) + Math.Pow(j-pos.Y,
        2);
    double radiusSQR = 50;
    if (distanceSQR < radiusSQR)
    {
5    //...
```

9.2   Full-Screen Pixel Modifications

Now that we know how to modify a single texture, we can take this a step further. Let's assume we have created a complicated scene involving multiple sprites at various layers. Suppose also that we now want to apply an effect (like the inverted circle from the previous example) across the entire scene.

The process to achieve this is fairly simple, even if it might seem a little complicated at first:

1. Store a reference to the current back buffer (render targets).

2. Create a temporary back buffer.

3. Draw the scene as usual to the temporary back buffer.

4. Restore the original render target.

5. Create a color array from the temporary back buffer.

6. Modify the color array (as before).

7. Create a texture from the modified color array.

8. Draw the modified texture to the screen.

In this case, we apply each of these as steps in the Draw function. The first step is to store a reference to the current back buffer. We call such a location a *render target*; normally, this is the back buffer. We can access the list of render targets as follows:

```
RenderTargetBinding[] tempBinding = GraphicsDevice.
    GetRenderTargets();
```

We now want to create a temporary location to which we can draw the scene. This acts just like the original back buffer, except it won't automatically send the results to the screen. To create a new render target and set it as the current location to draw the scene, we can add the following code. In this case, we assume we're drawing to a 1,280 × 720 screen.

```
int scr_width = 1280;
int scr_height = 720;

RenderTarget2D tempRenderTarget = new RenderTarget2D(
    GraphicsDevice, scr_width, scr_height);
GraphicsDevice.SetRenderTarget(tempRenderTarget);
```

Now we simply draw our scene as usual. In this case, I have left the details out of the code because we can apply this technique to any scene.

```
1   GraphicsDevice.Clear(Color.Black);
    spriteBatch.Begin(SpriteSortMode.BackToFront, BlendState.
       NonPremultiplied);
    //Draw sprite batch as usual.
    spriteBatch.End();
```

Once the scene is complete, we need to switch back to our original back buffer. We stored a reference to the back buffer in `tempBinding`, so we can call `SetRenderTargets` with that binding. Anything we draw after this point will be drawn to the screen, as we would expect.

```
1   GraphicsDevice.SetRenderTargets(tempBinding);
```

The scene we drew in the first step is still stored in `tempRenderTarget`. We can access it just as if it were a single texture of size $1{,}280 \times 720$. And as with our previous example, we can store the color data from the texture into an array of colors.

```
1   int scr_width = 1280;
    int scr_height = 720;
    Color[] arrayOfColor = new Color[scr_width * scr_height];
    tempRenderTarget.GetData<Color>(arrayOfColor);
```

We now have an array of colors as before. This time, however, instead of containing only a single sprite, the array contains the entire scene. As before, we can modify the individual colors of the array. In this case, let's apply a very simple blur effect.

The blur effect is achieved by replacing the current color with a blended average of the colors from either side of the current pixel color.

```
1   for (int j = 0; j < scr_height; j++)
      for (int i = 0; i < scr_width; i++)
      {
        int blurAmount = 5;
5
        int currElement = i + (scr_width * j);
        int prevElement = currElement - blurAmount;
        int nextElement = currElement + blurAmount;
        if (   ((currElement - blurAmount) > 0 )
10          && ((currElement + blurAmount) < (scr_width *
              scr_height)))
        {
          arrayOfColor[currElement].R =
          (byte)((arrayOfColor[currElement].R
                + arrayOfColor[prevElement].R
15              + arrayOfColor[nextElement].R) / 3.0f);
          arrayOfColor[currElement].G =
          (byte)((arrayOfColor[currElement].G
                + arrayOfColor[prevElement].G
                + arrayOfColor[nextElement].G) / 3.0f);
```

```
20      arrayOfColor[currElement].B =
        (byte)((arrayOfColor[currElement].B
              + arrayOfColor[prevElement].B
              + arrayOfColor[nextElement].B) / 3.0f);
      }
25    }
```

Now that we have blurred the color array, the next step is to create a new texture and push the color array into the new texture, creating a 1,280 × 720 texture that contains a blurred version of our image.

```
1   //Place color array into a texture
    Texture2D newTexture = new Texture2D(GraphicsDevice,
        scr_width, scr_height) ;
    newTexture.SetData<Color>(arrayOfColor);
```

As a last step, we now draw that new texture to the screen as one large sprite.

```
1   spriteBatch.Begin();
    spriteBatch.Draw(newTexture, Vector2.Zero, Color.White);
    spriteBatch.End();
```

However, blurring the entire scene isn't very appealing. Let's instead generate a different blur amount for each pixel, determined by the distance from the pixel to the center of the screen.

```
1   Vector2 center = new Vector2(scr_width / 2.0f, scr_height /
        2.0f);
    double maxDistSQR = Math.Sqrt(Math.Pow(center.X, 2)
                        + Math.Pow(center.Y, 2));

5   for (int j = 0; j < scr_height; j++)
      for (int i = 0; i < scr_width; i++)
      {
        double distSQR = Math.Sqrt(Math.Pow(i - center.X, 2)
                        + Math.Pow(j - center.Y, 2));
10
        int blurAmount = (int)Math.Floor(10 * distSQR /
            maxDistSQR);

        int currElement = i + (scr_width * j);
        int prevElement = currElement - blurAmount;
15      int nextElement = currElement + blurAmount;
        if (   ((currElement - blurAmount) > 0 )
            && ((currElement + blurAmount) < (scr_width *
                scr_height)))
        {
          arrayOfColor[currElement].R =
20        (byte)((arrayOfColor[currElement].R
                + arrayOfColor[prevElement].R
                + arrayOfColor[nextElement].R) / 3.0f);
```

```
        arrayOfColor[currElement].G =
        (byte)((arrayOfColor[currElement].G
25            + arrayOfColor[prevElement].G
              + arrayOfColor[nextElement].G) / 3.0f);
        arrayOfColor[currElement].B =
        (byte)((arrayOfColor[currElement].B
              + arrayOfColor[prevElement].B
30            + arrayOfColor[nextElement].B) / 3.0f);
    }
  }
```

The result of this modification can be seen in Figure 9.5.

This technique allows us to create some very impressive effects, but the load on the CPU is much higher than before, with upwards of a billion operations per second when applied to the 921,600 pixels that make up a 1,280 × 720 screen. With a billion operations per second, a 1-GHz CPU would be needed just to render the graphics. At this point, the average processor starts to get maxed out, and we haven't yet added any game play, physics simulation, or artificial intelligence.

By now, you probably see where we're going with this. With modern graphics processors, we can take the load of graphics processing off the CPU and hand it to the GPU. The GPU is a highly specialized processor designed to process graphics, specifically textures. And that just so happens to be exactly what we were trying to do with the CPU. The good news is that the GPU is mostly idle in 2D games, just waiting for us to make use of its processing power.

Figure 9.5. Snowmen blurred from the center.

9.3   What Is a Shader?

A *shader* is small program that runs on the graphics card. In 3D graphics, one of the primary tasks of a shader is to light (shade) the geometry of 3D objects. If this small shader program is applied to individual vertices in a 3D mesh, it is called a *vertex shader*.

Additionally, a shader can be written and applied to individual pixels. These shaders may be referred to as *pixel shaders* (sometimes called *fragment shaders* because they can be applied to a fragment of the screen). I prefer the term *pixel shader* because it emphasizes that the code is applied to individual pixels.

In the example in Section 9.2, we looped through every pixel in the color array, applying a small snippet of code to each pixel. This is the exact technique pixel shaders use as well; however, now the loop is already created for us and handled by the graphics card. In fact, because each pixel is modified independently, the shaders are well suited to parallel processing, and many GPUs will automatically divide the work among multiple processes.

9.4   Shader Languages

Because the shader is compiled for graphics hardware that is highly specialized, it needs to be written in a different and limited programming language. The two common programming languages for writing shader code are (1) *GLSL* (Graphics Library Shader Language), an open source language used when working with OpenGL; and (2) *HLSL* (High Level Shading Language), maintained by Microsoft and used when working with DirectX and XNA.

These two languages are very similar and resemble C code. The examples in this book are written in HLSL. In addition, because the graphics card in the Xbox 360 is compliant up to HLSL version 2.0, that is the standard we will use.

9.4.1   Shader Structure

The structure of a pixel shader is simple. By default, the shader has access to only a single texture (the array of colors representing the screen) and the current position of the pixel the shader will modify. The return value of a pixel shader is simply an RGBA color value.

An important thing to know when working with shaders is that the coordinate value for the current pixel is stored as a float value between 0 and 1. For example, the center pixel $(640, 360)$ of a screen that is 1280 pixels wide and 720 pixels high will be referenced as $(0.5, 0.5)$ in the shader.

This makes it easy to work within a shader because the screen resolution is irrelevant, but you need to remember to apply the appropriate screen ratio. For example, an attempt to render a circle on a square region of the shader will result in the circle being stretched out due to the aspect ratio when the image is applied to the screen.

In addition, shaders really must remain as small snippets of code. With HLSL Pixel Shader version 2.0, we are limited to 64 operations per pixel per pass.

In XNA, we can store the code as a text file (given the .fx extension) in the content folder. The XNA content pipeline will automatically compile the .fx shader code.

With all that in mind, let's look at the exact same radial blur function written in HLSL.

```
1    uniform extern texture ScreenTexture;

     sampler ScreenS = sampler_state
     {
5      Texture = <ScreenTexture>;
     };

     float4 PixelShaderFunction(float2 curCoord: TEXCOORD0) :
         COLOR
     {
10     float2 center = {0.5f, 0.5f};
       float maxDistSQR = 0.7071f; //precalulated sqrt(0.5f)

       float2 diff = abs(curCoord - center);
       float distSQR = length(diff);
15
       float blurAmount = (distSQR / maxDistSQR) / 100.0f;

       float2 prevCoord = curCoord;
       prevCoord[0] -= blurAmount;
20
       float2 nextCoord = curCoord;
       nextCoord[0] += blurAmount;

       float4 color = ((tex2D(ScreenS, curCoord)
25                   + tex2D(ScreenS, prevCoord)
                     + tex2D(ScreenS, nextCoord))/3.0f);

       return color;
     }
30   technique
     {
       pass P0
       {
         PixelShader = compile ps_2_0 PixelShaderFunction();
35     }
     }
```

In order to apply this effect, we first need to save the above code as `blur.fx` and add it to the content directory. Then we need to ensure the effect is added to the project and loaded as content.

```
Effect blurEffect;

//..

protected override void LoadContent()
{
  //..
  blurEffect = Content.Load<Effect>("blur");
  //..
}
```

Then in our Draw function, as before, we need to render to a temporary render target.

```
int scr_width = 1280;
int scr_height = 720;

RenderTargetBinding[] tempBinding = GraphicsDevice.
    GetRenderTargets();

RenderTarget2D tempRenderTarget = new RenderTarget2D(
    GraphicsDevice, scr_width, scr_height);
GraphicsDevice.SetRenderTarget(tempRenderTarget);

GraphicsDevice.Clear(Color.Black);
spriteBatch.Begin(SpriteSortMode.BackToFront, BlendState.
    NonPremultiplied);
//Draw sprite batch as usual.
spriteBatch.End();

GraphicsDevice.SetRenderTargets(tempBinding);
```

But this time, instead of generating a color array and modifying the individual elements, we allow the shader to do the work for us.

```
spriteBatch.Begin(SpriteSortMode.Immediate, BlendState.
    AlphaBlend);

//Apply shader code
blurEffect.CurrentTechnique.Passes[0].Apply();

//Draw previous render target to screen with shader applied
spriteBatch.Draw(tempRenderTarget, Vector2.Zero, Color.White)
    ;
spriteBatch.End();
```

On my development PC, the CPU version of this code caused my system to slow down to 4 fps, but by pushing the blur code onto the GPU, my game speed jumped by up to 60 fps.

9.4.2 Updating Shader Variables

Now that we have a great way to write code that will run on the GPU, we need one more option in order to write great effects. That is, we need to be able to pass values to the GPU.

Since the shader is running once for every pixel on the screen, it is convenient to update values within our shader code once a frame. That is, we update the shader in our Update function so that the next time we apply the shader to the scene in our Draw function, the updated variable has been set.

Let's start with a very simplistic example. This time, let's darken all the pixels by a specific value. In this case, the shader code will be the following:

```
//Listing for darken.fx

uniform extern texture ScreenTexture;

sampler ScreenS = sampler_state
{
   Texture = <ScreenTexture>;
};

float fBrightness;

float4 PixelShaderFunction(float2 curCoord: TEXCOORD0) : COLOR
{
   float4 color = tex2D(ScreenS, curCoord);

   color[0] *= fBrightness;
   color[1] *= fBrightness;
   color[2] *= fBrightness;

   return color;
}
technique
{
   pass P0
   {
      PixelShader = compile ps_2_0 PixelShaderFunction();
   }
}
```

Note that the parameter brightness is used but never set. This will happen within our main game code.

To do this, we create an effect parameter that is initialized along with the effect itself.

```
   public EffectParameter brightnessParam;
   public Effect darken;
```

At the same point when we load the Effect file (in the content loader), we also need to make the link between the variable inside the shader code and the variable as it exists within our main game.

```
//In Load Content:
darken = content.Load<Effect>("darken");
brightnessParam = darken.Parameters["fBrightness"];
```

Notice in this code that the quoted text fBrightness matches the variable name in the shader code exactly.

Now that the link has been made between brightnessParam (in the C# game code) and fBrightness (in the HLSL shader), we need only to set the value.

```
//In Update:

brightnessParam.SetValue(0.1f);
```

Finally, as before, if we apply the darkening shader when drawing, the result will be a darkened scene.

Now let's take it one step further by modifying the brightness parameter in each frame, as done in the following code:

```
double fPulse = Math.Abs(Math.Sin(gameTime.TotalGameTime.
    TotalMilliseconds / 500.0f));
brightnessParam.SetValue((float)fPulse);
```

With that, you have all the tools you need to create advanced graphical effects on the GPU. In the next section, I list a few ideas to get you started, but they really are just the beginning. My advice is to start simple and work your way up. It can take time to become comfortable with how and why you can use shaders to generate effects. But once you have a solid understanding, you'll realize just how powerful and beneficial GPU programming can be.

9.5   Pixel Shader Examples

Thus far, we have seen examples of modifying pixels to invert colors and to blur the scene. But what else can you do with a pixel shader? The answer is only limited by your imagination.

To get you thinking about the possibilities, a good place to start is with the filters that are available in raster graphics editors, such as Blender or Adobe Photoshop. This might include image distortion, for example, creating a moving ripple effect or a fisheye lens effect that follows the player. It might also include the ability to modify light, such as darkening an image and then reapplying light where lanterns are located.

In general, the web is a great source to find sample pixel shader code. However, I encourage you to explore the language of pixel shaders on your own before relying too heavily on web examples. Start with something very simple and work your way up.

9.5.1 Greyscale

A simple greyscale (Figure 9.6) can be achieved by replacing every component of RGB color with an average of the individual components. For example,

$$\text{red value} = \frac{\text{red value} + \text{green value} + \text{blue value}}{3}.$$

9.5.2 Lights and Fog of War

As another very simple example, we can create a light effect by simply darkening all the pixels outside a given radius around the player, with the result that the player can see only the immediate surroundings (Figure 9.7). This technique could also be used to illuminate only areas of the game that the player has already explored (Figure 9.8).

Games such as Sid Meier's *Civilization* [Meier and Shelley 91] use a similar effect to mimic the concept of a fog of war, the idea that any area where the player does not actively have units does not get updated on the map. This can be done by using a shader to slowly fade out the surrounding area.

Creating a series of lights potentially has two options. The first option is to pass an array of light location to the pixel shader, and then to use the distance to all individual light locations within the array to calculate the color at a given pixel. This approach might work for a few lights, but it becomes inefficient fairly quickly as we increase the number of lights.

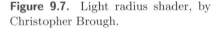

Figure 9.6. Shader renders scene in greyscale, by Thomas Francis.

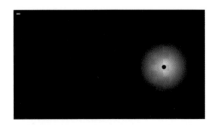

Figure 9.7. Light radius shader, by Christopher Brough.

Figure 9.8. Light radius shader (moments later), by Christopher Brough.

A better solution is to use a separate buffer and draw solid circular sprites in white, centered on the light locations. This second buffer can then be saved as a texture and used to create a kind of stencil. The colors of the two images are then combined, and the result is that wherever white has been added to the stencil, the scene is visible. Everywhere else is dark. (See Figure 9.9.)

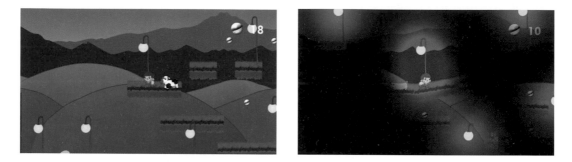

Figure 9.9. Advanced light shader with multiple lights sources, before (left) and after (right), by Thomas Francis.

Figure 9.10. Shader used to apply pixilation to menu text, by Thomas Francis.

9.5.3 Pixelation

By taking the average of the colors in an area of pixels and then replacing all the colors in that region with that average, we can create a simple *pixelation* effect.

Although pixelating a scene creates an interesting effect (see, for example, Figure 9.10), it is not necessarily very useful by itself. If the amount of the pixelation is modified dynamically (for example, by starting small and then increasing the pixelation effect), however, it be used as a transition between scenes.

In fact, many of these effects can be used dynamically. We look at more options for transitioning between scenes in Chapter 10.

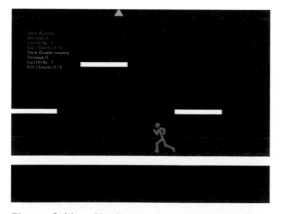

Figure 9.11. Shader used to create dynamic zoom by Gunther Fox in his unpublished game, *Super Stash Bros.*

9.5.4 Camera Zoom

Another simple shader effect is to scale up, such as doubling the area required to draw each pixel. If this process is used dynamically, it can be used as a *camera zoom*. This effect is employed in Gunther Fox's *Super Stash Bros* as seen in Figure 9.11.

Figure 9.12. Before applying fisheye shader, by Melissa Gill.

Figure 9.13. After applying fisheye shader, by Melissa Gill.

9.5.5 Fisheye

If, instead of setting the magnification as a constant value for every pixel (as in Figure 9.12), it is scaled up based on the distance from a center point, a fisheye lens effect is created (see Figure 9.13).

9.5.6 Ripple

Microsoft provides a great ripple example as part of the XNA Game Studio. This can be the basis for a great shock-wave or knock-back effect, perhaps as the result of an exploding shell from a tank.

9.5.7 Combined Effects

Combining effects may seem daunting, but it does not have to be. Depending on the effect, you may want to either swap render targets for each effect you want to implement or make use of multiple passes of the shader. Figure 9.14 shows the result of combining blurring and dimming.

9.5.8 Shader Editor

One of the frustrating things about working with shaders is that if something goes wrong, the screen will just go blank (or a default purple color will indicate an error). For obvious

Figure 9.14. Multiple shaders combine blur and decreasing light radius effects in Adam Reed's unpublished game, *Tunnel Vision*.

reasons, we don't currently have tools
that allow us to step through a shader debugger with breakpoints. Either
our code will work, or it won't. For that reason, I once again recommend
starting very simply (see the challenges at the end of this chapter to get
started).

When you are ready to take on more significant shader tasks, see the
companion website, http://www.2dGraphicsProgramming.com, for a link
to a real-time shader editor that will allow you to modify your shader code
and see the effect immediately. This ability can be quite helpful when
experimenting with new ideas.

Exercises: Challenges

Challenge 9.1. In order to become skilled with shaders, start small. Start
by writing a shader that will show only the red channel (set `color[1]` and
`color[2]` equal to zero).

Challenge 9.2. Create and implement a pixel shader that will invert all
the colors on the right side of the screen.

Challenge 9.3. Create and implement a pixel shader that will cause the
top-right portion of the screen to be displayed in greyscale.

Challenge 9.4. Create and implement a pixel shader that darkens the pixels based on their distance from the center of the screen.

Challenge 9.5. Create and implement a pixel shader that darkens the pixels around the mouse location. You have to pass the mouse location to the
shader and update the mouse location in every frame.

Challenge 9.6. Create and implement a pixel shader that distorts the background but does not affect the rest of your game. You can achieve this by
applying the shader and then drawing the rest of the sprites as usual.

Challenge 9.7. Combine two shader effects so that they are drawn simul-
taneously.

Chapter 10

Polish, Polish, Polish!

A little extra effort can go a long way in making a game feel professional. This chapter covers those little techniques that make good games look great.

Polish can be achieved with various combinations of animations, particles, and pixel shaders (see, for example, Figure 10.1). All that is required is the extra time to apply these techniques in creative and interesting ways. A great dynamic example of this is Denki's *Save the Day* (Figure 10.2), throughout which particles and animations are used to create exciting and active scenes.

Figure 10.1. In *Nuage*, Alex Tardif uses particles, shaders, and transitions effectively to create a relaxing game-like experience.

Figure 10.2. Concept art from Denki's *Save the Day.*

10.1   Transitions

Creating a simple *transition* between game states (for example, from the menu to the game) can make a surprisingly big difference in the quality of the game. Good transitions can make the game feel like a complete experience, even when the player is doing something as simple as pressing Pause.

In traditional film, transitions from scene to scene (as opposed to a straight cut) are important tools that have been used for decades. A commonly cited example is the wipe transition used by George Lucas in the *Star Wars* films [Lucas 77].

Transitions can be as simple as modifying the alpha value over time to fade to a background, or something significantly more complicated involving particle effects or a GPU shader. Various examples of simple transitions can be found in video editing software. Microsoft's Windows Live Movie Maker [Microsoft 00] is free software that includes a variety of transitions for digital video editing, including categories such as cross-fades, diagonals, dissolves, patterns and shapes, reveals, shatters, sweeps and curls, and wipes. All of these could be used as inspiration for the transitions in your game.

Recent games present many examples of great transitions. Both 8bit Games' *Elefunk* [8bit Games 08] and Proper Games' *Flock!* [Proper Games 09] use a transition reminiscent of the iconic shrinking circle employed at the end of Warner Bros.' *Looney Tunes*; however, instead of employing a circle, the transitions are accomplished with cutouts of elephants and sheep, respectively. Another example is the monkey head stencil as

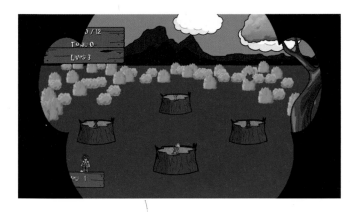

Figure 10.3. *Choco Says* [Trzcinski 11] monkey stencil transition effect.

demonstrated in the game *Choco Says* [Trzcinski 11] seen in Figure 10.3. In *Zombiez 8 My Cookiez* by Triple B Games [Triple B Games 10], the hands of cartoon zombies sweep across the screen.

10.1.1 Seamless Transitions

Note that although transitions are very important in creating a polished game, the average player should be completely unaware that anything unusual is occurring. The goal is to create a smooth shift from one game state to another. If the transition takes too long, players will become frustrated. With that in mind, the transition should occur very quickly, taking less than a second to complete.

10.1.2 Simple Linear Interpolation

In *aliEnd*, I implemented a simple transition between scenes that fades to and from a star field. The game employs an enumerated set of game states as well as an enumerated set of transition states. Fade-ins and fade-outs each take half a second.

```
public enum eGameStates
{
  STATE_NULL = 0,
  STATE_SETUP,
  STATE_FRONT_END,
  STATE_WARP_TO,
  STATE_MAIN_GAME,
  STATE_LEVEL_END,
  STATE_PAUSE,
  STATE_EXIT,
}
```

```
   public enum eTransitionStates
   {
15    FADE_IN = 0,
      FULL,
      FADE_OUT,
   }

20  private eGameStates m_eStateNext;
    private eTransitionStates m_eTransState;

    private double m_fTimeNext;
    private double m_fTimeMax = 0.5f;
25
    public byte fadeAlpha;
```

When the state is fading in or out, I drew the star field on top of the current scene by using the fadeAlpha value. Then in a State Update function, I modified the alpha value used to draw the star field.

```
1  public void Update(GameTime gameTime)
   {
     m_fTimeNext -= gameTime.ElapsedGameTime.TotalSeconds;

5    if (m_fTimeNext <= 0)
     {
         if (m_eTransState == eTransitionStates.FADE_IN)
         {
             m_eTransState = eTransitionStates.FULL;
10       }
         else if (m_eTransState == eTransitionStates.FADE_OUT)
         {
             m_eTransState = eTransitionStates.FADE_IN;
             eCurrentState = m_eStateNext;
15           m_fTimeNext = m_fTimeMax;
         }
         else
         {
             //Do nothing, timer not used until in transition
                 occuring
20       }
     }

     if (m_eTransState == eTransitionStates.FADE_IN)
     {
25     if (eCurrentState != eGameStates.STATE_LEVEL_END)
       {
         fadeAlpha = (byte)((m_fTimeNext / m_fTimeMax) * 255); //
             0->255
       }
     }
30   else if (m_eTransState == eTransitionStates.FADE_OUT)
```

```
   {
     if (m_eStateNext != eGameStates.STATE_LEVEL_END)
     {
       fadeAlpha = (byte)(((-m_fTimeNext / m_fTimeMax) * 255) +
           255); //255->0
35   }
   }
   else
   {
     fadeAlpha = 0;
40 }
 }
```

However, when it came time to implement the system, I identified that there were times when I wanted a transition to occur between game state changes but there were other times when I needed the state to change immediately. With that in mind, I created two functions for triggering state changes:

```
1  public void Set(eGameStates next)
   {
     if (next == eGameStates.STATE_NULL)
         return;

5
     if (m_eStateNext != next)
     {
       m_eStateNext = next;
       m_eTransState = eTransitionStates.FADE_OUT;
10     m_fTimeNext = m_fTimeMax;
     }
   }

   public void SetImmediate(eGameStates nextState,
       eTransitionStates nextTransition)
15 {
     if (nextState == eGameStates.STATE_NULL)
       return;

     m_eStateNext = eGameStates.STATE_NULL;
20   eCurrentState = nextState;
     m_eTransState = nextTransition;
     m_fTimeNext = 0.0f;
   }
```

This small block of code provided a very convenient system. For example, when the level was over, I could set the next state with one line of code (as shown below), and the fade-in and fade-out transitions would be implemented during the state change.

```
1  g_StateManager.Set(eGameStates.STATE_LEVEL_END);
```

10.1.3 Never a Static Screen

Like transitions, the use of progress bars or other graphics to indicate that work is occurring in the background can be a subtle but important part of user feedback. Just as for transitions, this can range from the simple to the complex.

In a game, it may take a few moments to load a file or wait for some process to complete. While this is going on, we never want the user to think that the game is hung up. In professional game development, publishers will set specific requirements related to this issue. For example, a console publisher may require that the game never have a static screen for more than three seconds.

Obviously, the first goal should be to limit the amount of time any code prevents the game from continuing. In many cases, asynchronous programming techniques will allow the game to continue while the would-be blocking operation is processed on a background thread. However, there are times when delay may be unavoidable, such as when querying data from a remote leader board across a slower Internet connection.

Figure 10.4. The *aliEnd* loading screen.

In *aliEnd*, while developing for the Xbox, this was never a significant issue. However, when I ported the game to the Android OS, I found that it took a few seconds to load the game assets. Even a few seconds can feel like an eternity for a player trying to start a game. Even though the asset loading was occurring in the background, it was important to update the user that progress was indeed happening.

For a simple solution (see Figure 10.4), as each asset loaded, I incremented a counter called `iLoadLoop`. I then added a dot to the word "Loading," so that on every fifth asset a subsequent dot is drawn to the screen, as in "Loading . . ."

```
1   spriteBatch.DrawString(g_FontManager.myFont, GameText.
        FRONTEND_LOADING, new Vector2(50, 50), myColor);
    for (int i = 0; i < iLoadLoop; i++)
    {
      if ((i % 5) == 0)
5       spriteBatch.DrawString(g_FontManager.myFont, ".", new
            Vector2(350 + (i * 10), 50), myColor);
    }
```

The disadvantage of using a series of dots is that the user has no idea how long the wait will be. A graphical progress bar that stretches a band of color based on the percentage complete might have provided a better solution. In this case, since the delay was only a few seconds, the text solution was sufficient.

For games in which the total time until completion is unknown (for example, when querying a remote network), something as simple as a spinning wheel will at least indicate that a process is occurring in the background.

10.2   Sinusoidal Movement

As discussed with animation techniques in Chapter 4, when we look at nature, we see that objects rarely move linearly. Objects will speed up and slow down instead of moving at a constant rate. In fact, when looking out across a landscape, we can see many objects that have a cyclic motion. This is as true for a leaf rolling on ocean waves as it is for the limbs of a tree as they blow in the wind.

By noticing this type of cyclic motion and then implementing similar movement into our games, we can create movement that seems more fluid and less robotic. This is easily done by using the sine formula.

Recall that the sine function returns a value between -1 and 1 based on the angle, which represents the y-value as you rotate around a unit circle. Likewise, the cosine function returns the x-value.

The following example demonstrates the difference in linear motion.

```
1   Texture2D whiteCircleTexture;

    float counter;

5   float    linearY;
    float     direction = 1;
    float     speed = 2.0f;

    //In LoadContent:

10
    whiteCircleTexture = Content.Load<Texture2D>("whiteCircle");

    //In Update:
    counter += ((float)gameTime.ElapsedGameTime.TotalSeconds *
        direction * speed);

15
    if (counter > (Math.PI * 0.5f))
    {
        counter = (float)(Math.PI * 0.5f);
        direction *= -1;
20  }
    if (counter < -(Math.PI * 0.5f))
    {
        counter = -(float)(Math.PI * 0.5f);
```

```
25      direction *= -1;
      }

      linearY = counter / (float)(Math.PI * 0.5f);

      //In Draw:
30
      GraphicsDevice.Clear(Color.Black);

      double scaledLin2 = (linearY * 256) + 300;

35    spriteBatch.Begin();
      spriteBatch.Draw(whiteCircleTexture,
                  new Vector2(790, scaledLin2),
                  Color.White);
      spriteBatch.End();
```

As you can see, this creates a very sharp bounce, similar to that used in early games such as Atari's *Pong* [Alcorn 72]. Although this may be the effect you're looking for, it can feel less natural than if the movement followed the sine curve.

Add the following code to the project to compare sinusoidal and linear movement.

```
1     float sinusoidalY;

      //In Update:

5     sinusoidalY = (float)Math.Sin(counter);

      //In Draw:

      double scaledSinY = (sinusoidalY * 256) + 300;
10
      //...
      spriteBatch.Draw(whiteCircleTexture,
                  new Vector2(360, scaledSinY),
                  Color.White);
15    //...
```

Notice that the frequency of motion is the same but sine provides a smoother motion.

Now let's see what happens when we restrict the y-values to being positive by adding the following to the end of the update function:

```
1     linearY = -Math.Abs(linearY);
      sinusoidalY = -Math.Abs(sinusoidalY);
```

Figure 10.5.
Sinusoidal motion.

Notice that the circle on the left (see Figure 10.5) bounces in a natural motion, whereas the circle on the right appears much more rigid. (You may need to take a moment and hold your hand over the right side and then the left in order to see the difference. The motion of the two together can play tricks on your eyes.)

In this simple example, we have applied sinusoidal motion to a sprite moving across the screen, but this could just as easily be applied to any value that changes over time. For example, if we want to create a pulsating light, modifying a color with the sine function can create a nice effect.

10.2.1   Look-Up Tables

One possible disadvantage to using sinusoidal motion is the computational cost of performing a sine calculation. This is not a significant issue on modern PCs, but it has the potential to be a performance issue when developing for mobile devices if sine is calculated thousands of times per frame.

A simple solution is to precalculate all the values of sine (for example, at every degree or tenth of a degree) and to store the results in a table or even a simple array. The resultant necessary memory usage would then be small compared to the potential for improved performance.

10.3   Splines

A *spline* is a curved line created from a mathematical relationship between multiple points. Consider the clear linear steps used to locate the pixels on a line between points. A spline uses the same concept, but instead of considering only two points, multiple control points are considered. The result of this nonlinear interpolation is a smoother curve.

Splines offer great opportunities to create additional types of nonlinear motion, mostly beyond the scope of this text. Various packages can help with the mathematics behind splines, and XNA comes with functions to quickly implement a variety via polynomial interpolations as part of the MathHelper library, including the Smooth-Step, Hermite, and CatmullRom methods.

The spline in Figure 10.6 was generated by calculating a y value for every x value between a series of points by using the following function, in which control points have varying weights, depending on how far along the x-axis the control point is from the current pixel:

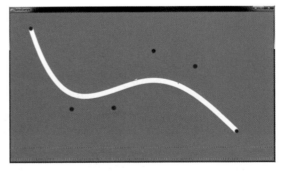

Figure 10.6. Spline with control points.

```
private float quadraticInterp(int xValue)
{
  float percentX = (xValue - m_controlPoints[0].X)
                    / (m_controlPoints[(m_controlPoints.Count-1)
                      ].X - m_controlPoints[0].X);

  float sum = 0;
  for (int i = 0; i < m_controlPoints.Count; i++)
  {
    float tempValue;
    if (i == 0 || i == (m_controlPoints.Count - 1))
        tempValue = 1;
    else
        tempValue = 1.5f *(m_controlPoints.Count - 1);

    sum += (float)(Math.Pow((1.0f - percentX), (
        m_controlPoints.Count - (i+1))))
        * (float)(Math.Pow((percentX), (i)))
        * tempValue
        * (float) (m_controlPoints[i].Y);
  }

  return sum;
}
```

The control points are simply a set of (x, y) coordinates that are generated and added at initialization.

```
public void Initialize()
{
  m_controlPoints.Add(new myVector2(100,  300));
  m_controlPoints.Add(new myVector2(300,  600));
  m_controlPoints.Add(new myVector2(500,  550));
  m_controlPoints.Add(new myVector2(700,  350));
  m_controlPoints.Add(new myVector2(900,  150));
  m_controlPoints.Add(new myVector2(1100, 700));
}
```

It is then simply a matter of stepping along the x-axis to generate a y-value for every x-value. The sprite is then drawn at that (x, y) point.

```
batch.Begin();
for (int x = 0; x <= 1280; x += xStep)
{
  float y = (int)quadraticInterp(x, m_controlPoints);
  batch.Draw(gameAssetSheet, new Vector2(x, y), Color.White);
}
batch.End();
```

The result is a much smoother and more polished result than could otherwise be achieved with such a limited set of data points.

Note that although this is a fairly crude implementation of what is possible with the use of splines, it serves to demonstrate the concept. In this example, all control points contribute to all y-values. Ideally, you would use only a limited number of control points (the four nearest). In addition, full implementation would calculate both x- and y-values based on how far you have proceeded down the spline.

Splines have various uses. As an example, a properly implemented spline in a tank game could be used as a basis for destructible terrain so that shells fired from a tank may lower a control point, resulting in large chunks blown from the soil. A more common use for splines is as paths for game objects. This results in smooth movement from a series of control points predefined by the designer.

10.4 Working with Your Artist

In general, the best polish is going to come while working closely with your artist(s). Your artist will not know what is possible with your code, and you probably won't have the same aesthetic and style sensibilities as your artist. Don't be afraid to prototype and try new things. Innovation often comes from experimentation, and not simply repeating what you have seen in the past.

Whenever possible, provide the ability for your artist to modify in-game values without requiring recompilation of the code in order to see the results. As a first step, you might create values that can be imported; however, the best results will come from providing an interface in which the artist can modify values at runtime and then be able to save those values once they are "just right."

Early in game development, you will want to allow large changes (orders of magnitude) to game values. For example, how well does the smoke effect look when it emits 10 particles per second? Then don't restrict your artist to increasing the emission value by just single digits; instead, allow the artist to crank it up to 100 particles per second, and then 1,000. If it then looks good at 1,000 particles per second but starts to cause frame-rate issues, try larger particles at lower speeds. The key is understanding the artist's goal and then using code to find creative ways to reach that goal.

10.5 Conclusion

The field of game development remains new and exciting, and we are still only experimenting and learning to tap into the potential of the kind of interactive experiences we can have with games. Young game developers have the opportunity to take games in a variety of new and exciting directions, especially now that the barriers to entry are lower than ever and the development platforms have never been more varied.

Someone once said to me that game development is still in a stage of progression similar to that of silent films. We have yet to reach our true potential as a creative medium.

The one overriding thought I want to leave with you is that you should learn as much as you can from traditional art, television, film, comics, and cartoons. Then work with your artist to apply those lessons, along with an attention to detail and polish that is worthy of this new media.

Exercises: Challenges

Challenge 10.1. Build a state transition system that allows for various transition effects.

Challenge 10.2. Add the ability to use a particle effect as a fade. For example, quickly fill the screen with bubbles. Once the image is completely covered, swap states and allow the bubbles to quickly and randomly pop, revealing the new game state.

Challenge 10.3. Create an artist interface to your transition system that allows your artist to modify and test transitions in real time. This can include the speed of the transition, the type of the transition, and the color used in fading or blending.

Challenge 10.4. Overload the sine function with your own look-up table. Analyze the performance against the original sine function.

Challenge 10.5. Research and implement sprite movement along splines by using the built-in packages for Hermite and Catmull-Rom. Compare the results.

Part IV

Appendices

Appendix A

Math Review: Geometry

A.1 Cartesian Mathematics

In the *Cartesian coordinate system*, values of x are measured along a horizontal line and values of y are measured along a vertical line. The resultant grid space allows us to chart the location of objects.

On the computer, screen coordinates are measured from either the top-left or bottom-left corner, depending on the graphics API. In XNA and DirectX, the position $(0,0)$ is located in the top-left corner of the screen, with y increasing in value as we move downward. In OpenGL, the position $(0,0)$ is located in the bottom-left corner of the screen, with y increasing in value as we move upward.

A.2 Line

The equation of a *line*, where m is the slope and b is the offset from the x-axis, is

$$y = mx + b.$$

A.3 Circle

A *circle* can be described in terms of the following relationship between x and y, where r is the radius and the circle is centered on the origin $(0,0)$:

$$x^2 + y^2 = r^2.$$

A *unit circle* is the circle of radius 1 centered at the origin $(0,0)$. Thus, its equation is

$$x^2 + y^2 = 1.$$

A.4   Pythagorean Theorem

From the unit circle, we can derive the *Pythagorean theorem*, where $x = \frac{a}{c}$ and $y = \frac{b}{c}$:

$$c^2 = a^2 + b^2.$$

A.5   Distance

As a result, we can calculate the *distance between two points* as

$$c = \sqrt{(\Delta x)^2 + (\Delta y)^2},$$

or more specifically, between points A and B as

$$c = \sqrt{(B_x - A_x)^2 + (B_y - A_y)^2}.$$

A.6   Distance Squared

Often, we need to compare two distances—for example, to find whether the distance from A to B is less than the distance from C to D.

As a first pass at answering this question, we might write code to perform the following comparison:

$$\text{Is } \sqrt{(B_x - A_x)^2 + (B_y - A_y)^2} < \sqrt{(D_x - C_x)^2 + (D_y - C_y)^2}?$$

It should be clear that simplification of this calculation would allow us to perform the same comparison without the need to calculate the square root (resulting in improved performance). So, our code should instead perform the following (squared) comparison:

$$\text{Is } (B_x - A_x)^2 + (B_y - A_y)^2 < (D_x - C_x)^2 + (D_y - C_y)^2?$$

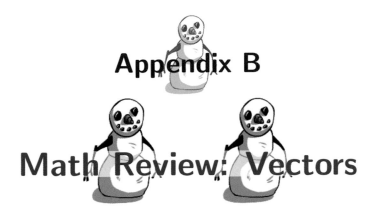

Appendix B

Math Review: Vectors

Courtesy of Dr. Scott Stevens

This appendix presents a review of vectors and the geometry of 2D space. We consider a *vector* as a directed line segment that has a length and a direction. This vector can be situated anywhere in space. As such, a single vector actually describes infinitely many possible directed line segments starting at any location in our geometry. Because of this ambiguity, we generally consider a vector to start at the origin.

Understanding that we can divide the vector into component form allows us to easily perform the mathematical operations of addition and subtraction on those vectors. This component-based use of vectors is the basis for position and motion in our graphics systems.

B.1 Vectors and Notation

B.1.1 Directed Line Segment

A *directed line segment* from an initial point P to a terminal point Q is denoted $\overrightarrow{PQ}$. It has a length (or magnitude) denoted by $||\overrightarrow{PQ}||$. Directed line segments with the same length and direction are called *equivalent*. For any directed line segment, there are infinitely many equivalent directed line segments.

A *vector* is a standardized representation of all equivalent line segments.

B.1.2   Component Form of a Vector

If $\overrightarrow{v}$ is a vector with initial point at the origin $(0,0)$ and terminal point (x,y), then the component form of $\overrightarrow{v}$ is $\overrightarrow{v} = \langle x, y \rangle$. Note the angled brackets.

If $\overrightarrow{v}$ is a vector defined by the directed line segment with initial point $P = (P_1, P_2)$ and terminal point $Q = (Q_1, Q_2)$, then the component form of this vector is defined by $\overrightarrow{v} = \langle Q_1 - P_1, Q_2 - P_2 \rangle$. This has the geometric effect of taking the original directed line segment and translating it to an equivalent one with its initial point at the origin.

Example: Given $P = (-1, 3)$ and $Q = (3, -5)$, find $\overrightarrow{v} = \overrightarrow{PQ}$.

Answer: The vector is $\overrightarrow{PQ} = \langle 3 - (-1), -5 - 3 \rangle = \langle 4, -8 \rangle = \overrightarrow{v}$.

B.1.3   Vector Notation

- Vectors are denoted in two different ways. In typeset material, a vector is generally denoted by a lowercase, boldface letter such as $\mathbf{u}$, $\mathbf{v}$, or $\mathbf{w}$. When written by hand, the arrow notation is used, such as $\overrightarrow{u}$, $\overrightarrow{v}$, or $\overrightarrow{w}$.

- Components of a vector are generally given in terms of the vector variable, such as $\mathbf{u} = \langle u_1, u_2 \rangle$ and $\mathbf{v} = \langle v_1, v_2 \rangle$.

B.2   Vector Comparison

B.2.1   Equivalent Vectors

Two vectors are considered *equivalent* if they have the same length and direction. This results in the two vectors having identical components when written in component form. Thus, if $\mathbf{u} = \langle u_1, u_2 \rangle$ and $\mathbf{v} = \langle v_1, v_2 \rangle$, then

$$\mathbf{u} = \mathbf{v} \iff u_1 = v_1 \text{ and } u_2 = v_2.$$

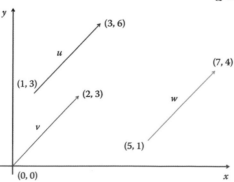

Example: Verify that the three vectors in the figure here are equivalent.

Answer: The vectors in component form are

$$\mathbf{u} = \langle 3 - 1, 6 - 3 \rangle = \langle 2, 3 \rangle,$$
$$\mathbf{v} = \langle 2 - 0, 3 - 0 \rangle = \langle 2, 3 \rangle,$$
$$\mathbf{w} = \langle 7 - 5, 4 - 1 \rangle = \langle 2, 3 \rangle.$$

Since the components are identical, these vectors are equivalent.

B.2.2   Scalar Multiplication of Vectors

If k is a scalar (real number) and $\mathbf{u} = \langle u_1, u_2 \rangle$ is a vector, then

$$k\mathbf{u} = \langle ku_1, ku_2 \rangle .$$

The geometric interpretation of scalar multiplication of vectors is that if the length of the vector is multiplied by $|k|$ and k is negative, then the direction of the vector switches. Thus, if $k = -1$, $k\mathbf{u}$ looks just like $\mathbf{u}$, only pointing in the opposite direction.

B.2.3   Parallel Vectors

Two vectors are *parallel* if they are scalar multiples of each other, $\mathbf{v} = k\mathbf{u}$. If $\mathbf{u} = \langle u_1, u_2 \rangle$ and $\mathbf{v} = \langle v_1, v_2 \rangle$ then,

$$\mathbf{u} \text{ is parallel to } \mathbf{v} \iff v_1 = k\,u_1 \text{ and } v_2 = k\,u_2.$$

Example: Verify that the two vectors in the figure here are parallel.

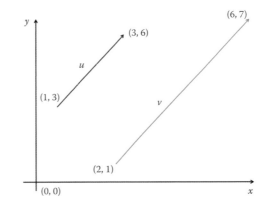

Answer: The vectors in component form are

$$\mathbf{u} = \langle 3 - 1, 6 - 3 \rangle = \langle 2, 3 \rangle ,$$
$$\mathbf{v} = \langle 6 - 2, 7 - 1 \rangle = \langle 4, 6 \rangle .$$

Notice that

$$\frac{v_1}{u_1} = \frac{4}{2} = 2 \text{ and } \frac{v_2}{u_2} = \frac{6}{3} = 2,$$

so $\mathbf{v} = 2\mathbf{u}$, and the vectors are parallel.

B.2.4   Application: Collinear Points

To determine if three points P, Q, and R are *collinear* (lie in a line), check to see whether the vectors $\overrightarrow{PQ}$ and $\overrightarrow{PR}$ are parallel. If they are, then the three points are collinear.

Example: Verify that the points $P = (1, 3)$, $Q = (3, 6)$, and $R = (9, 15)$ are collinear.

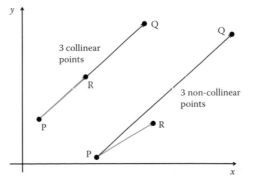

Answer:

$$\overrightarrow{PQ} = \langle 3 - 1, 6 - 3 \rangle - \langle 2, 3 \rangle$$
$$\overrightarrow{PR} = \langle 9 - 1, 15 - 3 \rangle = \langle 8, 12 \rangle$$

Since $\overrightarrow{PR} = 4\,\overrightarrow{PQ}$, these vectors are parallel and the points are collinear.

B.3   Length, Addition, and Subtraction

B.3.1   Length of a Vector

A vector in component form $\mathbf{v} = \langle v_1, v_2 \rangle$ has *length* (or *magnitude* or *norm*) given by

$$||\mathbf{v}|| = \sqrt{v_1^2 + v_2^2}$$

A vector of zero length is called the *zero vector*, $\mathbf{0} = \langle 0, 0 \rangle$.

Example: Find the length of the vector from $P = (-1, 3)$ to $Q = (4, 15)$.

Answer: $\overrightarrow{PQ} = \langle 5, 12 \rangle$, and $||\overrightarrow{PQ}|| = \sqrt{5^2 + 12^2} = \sqrt{169} = 13$.

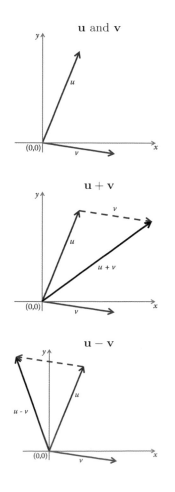

B.3.2   Vector Addition

Vector addition is performed component by component:

$$\mathbf{u} + \mathbf{v} = \langle u_1 + v_1, u_2 + v_2 \rangle .$$

The geometric interpretation of vector addition (known as *tip-to-tail*) is to align the end (tip) of $\mathbf{u}$ with the beginning (tail) of $\mathbf{v}$ and then connect the tail of $\mathbf{u}$ with the tip of $\mathbf{v}$ to create $\mathbf{u} + \mathbf{v}$. See the figure on the left.

Note that if $\mathbf{u}$ and $\mathbf{v}$ represent forces, then $\mathbf{u} + \mathbf{v}$ is called the *resultant force*.

B.3.3   Vector Subtraction

Vector subtraction is also performed component by component:

$$\mathbf{u} - \mathbf{v} = \langle u_1 - v_1, u_2 - v_2 \rangle .$$

The geometric interpretation of vector subtraction (know as *tip-to-tip*) is to align the tip of $\mathbf{u}$ with the tip of $\mathbf{v}$ and then connect the tail of $\mathbf{u}$ to the tail of $\mathbf{v}$ to create $\mathbf{u} - \mathbf{v}$. See the figure on the left. It might be easier just to picture $\mathbf{u} - \mathbf{v}$ as $\mathbf{u} + (-\mathbf{v})$.

B.4 Unit Vectors and Normalizing a Vector

A *unit vector* is a vector with length 1. The unit vector $\mathbf{u}$ in the direction of $\mathbf{v}$ is given by

$$\mathbf{u} = \frac{1}{||\mathbf{v}||}\,\mathbf{v} = \frac{\mathbf{v}}{||\mathbf{v}||}.$$

This is called *normalizing* the vector $\mathbf{v}$.

Example: Find the unit vector ($\mathbf{u}$) in the direction of $\mathbf{v} = \langle -3, 2 \rangle$. That is, normalize $\mathbf{v}$.

Answer: $||\mathbf{v}|| = \sqrt{(-3)^2 + 2^2} = \sqrt{13}$. So, $\mathbf{u} = \frac{1}{\sqrt{13}}\mathbf{v} = \left\langle \frac{-3}{\sqrt{13}}, \frac{2}{\sqrt{13}} \right\rangle$.

Example: Given points $P = (2,3)$ and $Q = (7,12)$, find point S such that S is 4 units from P in the direction of Q.

Answer: The strategy is to normalize $\overrightarrow{PQ}$ and multiply it by 4 to get $\overrightarrow{PS}$, and then add $\overrightarrow{PS}$ to point P to get S. (Mathematically speaking, you can't add a vector to a point without defining a new operation, but we allow it here for practical purposes.) So,

$$\overrightarrow{PQ} = \langle 7 - 2, 12 - 3 \rangle = \langle 5, 9 \rangle,$$

$$||\overrightarrow{PQ}|| = \sqrt{5^2 + 9^2} = \sqrt{106}.$$

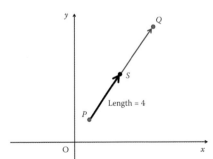

Thus,

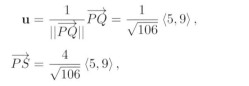

$$\mathbf{u} = \frac{1}{||\overrightarrow{PQ}||}\,\overrightarrow{PQ} = \frac{1}{\sqrt{106}}\,\langle 5, 9 \rangle,$$

$$\overrightarrow{PS} = \frac{4}{\sqrt{106}}\,\langle 5, 9 \rangle,$$

which leads to

$$S = P + \overrightarrow{PS} = (2,3) + \frac{4}{\sqrt{106}}\,\langle 5, 9 \rangle \approx (3.94, 6.50).$$

B.5 Vector Properties

Let $\mathbf{u}$, $\mathbf{v}$, and $\mathbf{w}$ be vectors, and let c and d be scalars. Then we can define the properties of vectors as follows:

1. **Commutative property:** $\mathbf{u} + \mathbf{v} = \mathbf{v} + \mathbf{u}$.

2. **Associative property:** $\mathbf{u} + (\mathbf{v} + \mathbf{w}) = (\mathbf{u} + \mathbf{v}) + \mathbf{w}$.

3. **Distributive properties:**
    - $(c + d)\,\mathbf{u} = c\,\mathbf{u} + d\,\mathbf{u}$,
    - $c(\mathbf{u} + \mathbf{v}) = c\,\mathbf{u} + c\,\mathbf{v}$.

4. **Additive identity:** $\mathbf{0} = \langle 0, 0 \rangle$ is called the zero vector and $\mathbf{u} + \mathbf{0} = \mathbf{u}$.

5. **Multiplicative identity:** $1\,\mathbf{u} = \mathbf{u}$.

6. **Additive inverse:** $\mathbf{u} + (-\mathbf{u}) = \mathbf{0}$.

7. **Zero property:** $0\,\mathbf{u} = \mathbf{0}$.

8. $c(d\,\mathbf{u}) = cd\,\mathbf{u}$.

9. $||k\mathbf{u}|| = |k|\,||\mathbf{u}||$.

10. **Triangle inequality:** $||\mathbf{u} + \mathbf{v}|| \leq ||\mathbf{u}|| + ||\mathbf{v}||$.

B.6   Standard Unit Vectors and Polar Representation

B.6.1   Standard Unit Vectors

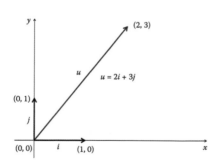

The *standard unit vectors* (basis vectors) in 2D space are $\mathbf{i} = \langle 1, 0 \rangle$ and $\mathbf{j} = \langle 0, 1 \rangle$.

Any vector $\mathbf{u} = \langle u_1, u_2 \rangle$ can be expressed as a linear combination of $\mathbf{i}$ and $\mathbf{j}$ by

$$\mathbf{u} = u_1\,\mathbf{i} + u_2\,\mathbf{j}.$$

Here, u_1 is called the *horizontal* component of $\mathbf{u}$ and u_2 is called the *vertical* component of $\mathbf{u}$.

Example: Express the vector $\mathbf{u} = \langle 2, 3 \rangle$ as a linear combination of the standard unit vectors $\mathbf{i}$ and $\mathbf{j}$.

Answer: $\mathbf{u} = \langle 2, 3 \rangle = 2\,\mathbf{i} + 3\,\mathbf{j}$. Yes, it's that simple.

B.6.2 Polar Representation of Vectors

If $\mathbf{u}$ is a vector with length $||\mathbf{u}||$ that makes a (counterclockwise) angle θ from the positive x-axis, then

$$\mathbf{u} = ||\mathbf{u}|| \cos \theta \, \mathbf{i} + ||\mathbf{u}|| \sin \theta \, \mathbf{j} = ||\mathbf{u}|| \left\langle \cos \theta, \sin \theta \right\rangle.$$

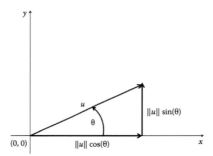

Example: Suppose the vector $\mathbf{u}$ has length 2 and makes an angle of $60°$ with the positive x-axis. Express $\mathbf{u}$ as a linear combination of $\mathbf{i}$ and $\mathbf{j}$, and then give the component form of $\mathbf{u}$.

Answer: Since the vector must have length 2, we know that $||\mathbf{u}|| = 2$. Also, $60° = \pi/3$ radians.

Expressed as a linear combination of $\mathbf{i}$ and $\mathbf{j}$,

$$\begin{aligned}
\mathbf{u} &= ||\mathbf{u}|| \, \cos \theta \, \mathbf{i} + ||\mathbf{u}|| \, \sin \theta \, \mathbf{j} \\
&= 2 \, \cos (\pi/3) \, \mathbf{i} + 2 \, \sin (\pi/3) \mathbf{j} \\
&= 2 \, \frac{1}{2} \, \mathbf{i} + 2 \, \frac{\sqrt{3}}{2} \, \mathbf{j} \\
&= \mathbf{i} + \sqrt{3} \, \mathbf{j}.
\end{aligned}$$

Expressed in component form, $\mathbf{u} = \left\langle 1, \sqrt{3} \right\rangle$.

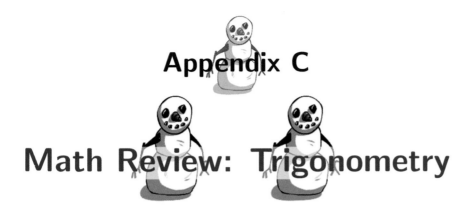

Appendix C

Math Review: Trigonometry

Courtesy of Dr. Scott Stevens

In this appendix, we start briefly with some triangle trigonometry and then move onto unit-circle trigonometry and trigonometry as periodic functions of a continuous variable. We end with how to create circles and ellipses and a brief description of the tangent function.

C.1   Triangle Trigonometry

Consider the right triangle shown here. We focus here on three trigonometric functions: cosine (cos), sine (sin), and tangent (tan). These functions are defined in terms of an angle, θ (*theta*) as follows:

$$\sin(\theta) = \frac{a}{c} = \frac{\text{adjacent edge}}{\text{hypotenuse}},$$

$$\cos(\theta) = \frac{b}{c} = \frac{\text{opposite edge}}{\text{hypotenuse}},$$

$$\tan(\theta) = \frac{a}{b} = \frac{\text{adjacent edge}}{\text{opposite edge}}.$$

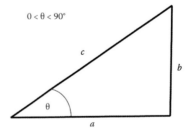

There are quite a few things you can determine from these relations:

- If you know two of the side lengths, you can utilize Pythagorean's theorem ($a^2 + b^2 = c^2$) to get the third side length and hence all of the trigonometric functions of all of the angles. Through inverse trigonometric functions, you can get both of the unknown angles as well.

- If you know θ and one side length, you can, through various identities and inverse trigonometric functions, determine the other two side lengths and all of the trigonometric functions of that angle and the other angle.

- Once you include the law of sines and/or the law of cosines, you can start to play with non-right triangles as well.

C.2 Unit-Circle Trigonometry

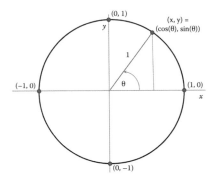

Consider the circle centered at $(0,0)$ in the Cartesian plane with radius equal to one. Now we define our trigonometric functions in terms of the angle traced out by the ray moving counterclockwise around the circle.

For every point (x, y) on the unit circle,

$$\cos(\theta) = x,$$
$$\sin(\theta) = y,$$
$$\tan(\theta) = \frac{y}{x}.$$

Here are a few things to notice:

- These match the triangle trigonometric functions when $0 < \theta < 90°$ (because $c = 1$).

- We can use any angle we want, even negative angles.

- It is immediately obvious what $\cos(\theta)$ and $\sin(\theta)$ are for $\theta = 0$, 90, 180, 270, 360, ...

- It is obvious that the sine and cosine functions repeat themselves after every full rotation. In other words, these functions are *periodic*.

C.2.1 Radians

Instead of measuring θ in degrees, we now measure it with respect to the arc length traced out by the unit circle to the point (x, y). This type of angle measurement is called *radians*. One full revolution is $360° = 2\pi$ radians. A half a revolution is $180° = \pi$ radians. A quarter revolution is $90° = \pi/2$ radians. Almost all calculators and software calculate trigonometric functions assuming the argument is in radians.

C.2.2 Converting between Degrees and Radians

If r is radians and d is degrees, then

$$d = \frac{180}{\pi} r \quad \text{and} \quad r = \frac{\pi}{180} d.$$

C.3 Trigonometry as a Collection of Periodic Functions

Here we look at sine and cosine as periodic functions of a continuous variable. (We will save tangent for later.) Consider the unit circle as the angle (now denoted by t in radians) goes around the circle in a counterclockwise direction as shown. If we track $x = \cos(t)$ and $y = \sin(t)$ to plot these functions, we get the following periodic graphs:

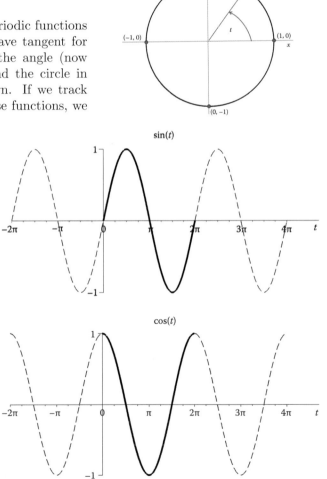

$\sin(t)$ has period 2π.

For $k = $ any integer,

$\sin(t + k\,2\pi) = \sin(t),$

$\sin(k\,\pi) = 0,$

$\sin\left(\left(\dfrac{4k+1}{2}\right)\pi\right) = 1,$

$\sin\left(\left(\dfrac{4k-1}{2}\right)\pi\right) = -1.$

$\cos(t)$ has period 2π.

For any integer k,

$\cos(t + k\,2\pi) = \cos(t),$

$\cos(2k\,\pi) = 1,$

$\cos((2k+1)\,\pi) = -1,$

$\cos\left(\left(\dfrac{2k+1}{2}\right)\pi\right) = 0.$

C.4   The Tangent Function

The *tangent* function is defined in terms of the sine and cosine functions by

$$\tan(x) = \frac{\sin(x)}{\cos(x)}.$$

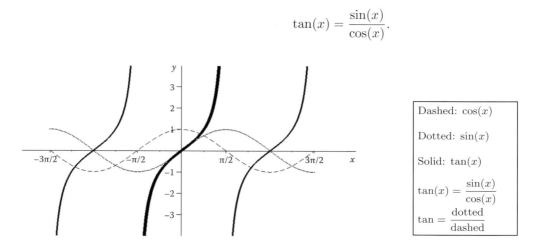

Dashed: $\cos(x)$

Dotted: $\sin(x)$

Solid: $\tan(x)$

$$\tan(x) = \frac{\sin(x)}{\cos(x)}$$

$$\tan = \frac{\text{dotted}}{\text{dashed}}$$

Two properties of the tangent function can be seen in its graph. Unlike sine and cosine, tangent has a period of π rather than 2π. Also, the tangent function is undefined at $\frac{2k+1}{2}\pi$ for all integers k (i.e., when $\cos = 0$), and the graph of $\tan(x)$ has vertical asymptotes at these locations.

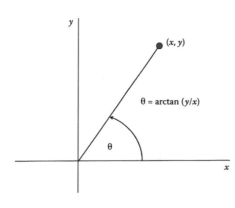

The *arctangent* (arctan) function is the inverse of the tangent function (sometimes denoted $\tan^{-1}$):

$$-\pi/2 < \arctan \leq \pi/2.$$

Most calculators and software contain an `atan2(y,x)` function, which resolves all of the issues of using the arctan function when $x \leq 0$:

$$-\pi < \texttt{atan2(y,x)} \leq \pi.$$

C.5 Translations and Transforms of Trigonometric Functions

C.5.1 Horizontal and Vertical Translations

$$y = \cos(x - \phi) + B \quad \text{and} \quad y = \sin(x - \phi) + B.$$

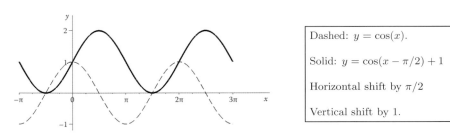

Dashed: $y = \cos(x)$.

Solid: $y = \cos(x - \pi/2) + 1$

Horizontal shift by $\pi/2$

Vertical shift by 1.

C.5.2 Amplitude Changes

$$y = A \cos(x) \quad \text{and} \quad y = A \sin(x),$$

where A is the amplitude.

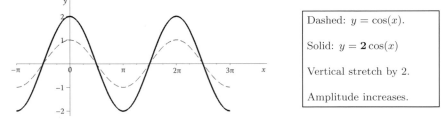

Dashed: $y = \cos(x)$.

Solid: $y = \mathbf{2}\cos(x)$

Vertical stretch by 2.

Amplitude increases.

C.5.3 Period (Frequency) Changes

$$y = \cos(\omega x) \quad \text{and} \quad y = \sin(\omega x),$$

where the period $= \frac{2\pi}{\omega}$.

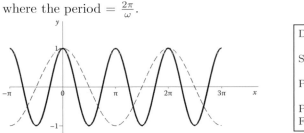

Dashed: $y = \cos(x)$.

Solid: $y = \cos(\mathbf{2}x)$

Period $= (2\pi/\mathbf{2}) = \pi$

Period decreases and Frequency increases.

C.6   Circles and Ellipses

Getting the graph of a circle in terms of $y = f(x)$ is tricky, and defining the graph of an ellipse is even trickier. These curves are much easier to create when you define them as a set of trigonometric parametric equations. In a *parametric curve*, the values of x and y are both determined in terms of another variable (parameter) usually denoted as t or θ.

An ellipse with center (x_0, y_0), x radius of r_x, and y radius of r_y is defined by

$$x(t) = x_0 + r_x \cos(t), \quad y = y_0 + r_y \sin(t), \quad t \in [0, 2\pi].$$

To make partial ellipses and circles, let the parameter range over an appropriate subset.

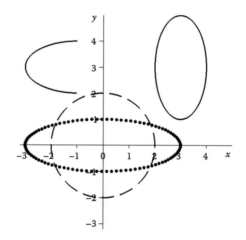

Dashed (circle)	Dotted (ellipse)	Solid (ellipse)	Solid (half-ellipse)
$x(t) = 2\cos(t)$	$x(t) = 3\cos(t)$	$x(t) = 3 + \cos(t)$	$x(t) = -1 + 2\cos(t)$
$y(t) = 2\sin(t)$	$y(t) = \sin(t)$	$y(t) = 3 + 2\sin(t)$	$y(t) = 3 + \sin(t)$
$t \in [0, 2\pi]$	$t \in [0, 2\pi]$	$t \in [0, 2\pi]$	$t \in [\pi/2, 3\pi/2]$

Bibliography

[8bit Games 08] 8bit Games. *Elefunk*. Xbox 360, PS3, 2008.

[Alcorn 72] Allan Alcorn. *Pong*. Atari Inc., Arcade, 1972.

[Blizzard North 96] Blizzard North. *Diablo*. Blizzard Entertainment, Microsoft Windows, 1996.

[Capcom 89] Capcom. *Final Fight*. Capcom, Arcade, 1989.

[Contestabile 12] Giordano Contestabile. "One Year of Bejewled Blitz—Learning to Expect the Unexpected." Smartphone and Tablet Games Summit, Game Developer Conference Online, San Francisco, CA, 2012.

[Davis and Lee 82] Warren Davis and Jeff Lee. *Q*bert*. Gottlieb, Arcade, 1982.

[Disney 57] Walt Disney Animation Studios. *Disneyland, Tricks of Our Trade*. Television special, Walt Disney Productions, 1957.

[Disney 91] Walt Disney Animation Studios. *Beauty and the Beast*. Feature-length animated film, Walt Disney Pictures, 1991.

[Disney 94] Walt Disney Animation Studios. *The Lion King*. Feature-length animated film, Walt Disney Pictures, 1994.

[Firaxis 09] Firaxis. *Civilization Revolution*. 2K Games, iOS, 2009.

[Fox 10] Gunther Fox. *Super Stash Bros*. http://www.guntherfox.com/portSSB.html, 2010.

[Garriott 81] Richard Garriott. *Ultima I: The First Age of Darkness*. Origin Systems, Apple II, 1981.

[Garriott 90] Richard Garriott. "Richard 'Lord British' Garriott speaks about ULTIMA." Cassette tape with *ULTIMA VI*, Special Edition, ORIGIN Systems, Inc., 1990.

[Get Set Games Inc. 11] Get Set Games Inc. *Mega Jump*. Apple Inc., iOS, 2011.

[Halfbrick Studios 10] Halfbrick Studios. *Fruit Ninja*. Halfbrick Studios, iOS, 2010.

[Harmonix 05] Harmonix. *Guitar Hero*. Activision, Xbox 360, PS3, 2005.

[Kirby 54] John Joshua Kirby. "Dr. Brook Taylor's Method of Perspective made Easy both in Theory and Practice." Pamphlet, 1754.

[Looking Glass Studios 98] Looking Glass Studios. *Thief: The Dark Project.* Eidos Interactive, PC, 1998.

[Lucas 77] George Lucas. *Star Wars.* Film, Lucasfilm Ltd, 1977.

[Lutz 10] Daniel Lutz. *Colorbind.* Self-published, iOS, 2010.

[Meier and Shelley 91] Sid Meier and Bruce Shelley. *Civilization.* MicroProse, cross-platform, 1991.

[Microsoft 00] Microsoft. "Windows Live Movie Maker." Freeware, 2000.

[Miyamoto and Tezuka 85] Shigeru Miyamoto and Takashi Tezuka. *Super Mario Bros.* Nintendo, Nintendo Entertainment System, 1985.

[Miyamoto and Tezuka 86] Shigeru Miyamoto and Takashi Tezuka. *The Legend of Zelda.* Nintendo, Nintendo Entertainment System, 1986.

[Nishikado 78] Tomohiro Nishikado. *Space Invaders.* Taito, Arcade, 1978.

[Pile 12] John Jr Pile. *aliEnd.* Self-published, Android, 2012.

[PopCap Games 07] PopCap Games. *Peggle.* PopCap Games, cross-platform, 2007.

[PopCap Games 09] PopCap Games. *Plants vs. Zombies.* PopCap Games, cross-platform, 2009.

[Proper Games 09] Proper Games. *Flock!* Capcom, Xbox 360, PS3, PC, 2009.

[Rasmussen 05] Michael Rasmussen. "Anatomy of a 2D Side-Scroller." Game Design Lecture, Game Developer Conference, San Francisco, CA, 2005.

[Rovio Entertainment 09] Rovio Entertainment. *Angry Birds.* Rovio Entertainment, iOS, 2009.

[Seckel 07] Al Seckel. *Masters of Deception: Escher, Dali & the Artists of Optical Illusion.* New York: Sterling Publishing Co., Inc., 2007.

[Stevens 12] Scott Stevens. *Matrices, Vectors, and 3D Math: A Game Programming Approach with MATLAB.* Cambridge, MA: Worldwide Center of Mathematics, 2012.

[The Behemoth 08] The Behemoth. *Castle Crashers.* Microsoft Game Studios, XBLA, 2008.

[Thomas and Johnston 81] Frank Thomas and Ollie Johnston. *The Illusion of Life: Disney Animation.* New York: Hyperion, 1981.

[Triple B Games 10] Triple B Games. *Zombiez 8 My Cookiez.* Tripple B Games, Xbox Live Indie Games, 2010.

[Trzcinski 11] Erin Trzcinski. *Choco Says.* http://www.erintrzcinski.com/#! choco-says, 2011.

[White 05] David White. *Battle for Wesnoth.* Self-published, cross-platform, 2005.

[Zynga Dallas 11] Zynga Dallas. *CastleVille.* Zynga, Adobe Flash, 2011.

[Zynga 09] Zynga. *FarmVille.* Zynga, Adobe Flash, 2009.

Glossary

alpha value A numeric representation of the effective transparency of an object. When stored as a byte, values range from 0 (completely transparent) to 255 (completely opaque). *21*

aspect ratio The proportional relationship between the width and height of an image commonly expressed in two numbers separated by a colon, as in 4:3. *26*

atlas A programmatically generated sprite sheet. *37, 49*

bit Short for *binary digit*, the smallest unit of information stored on a computer, having the value 1 or 0. *15*

bitmap A 2D array of pixels. Each member of the array stores the color of the corresponding pixel. This is not to be confused with "Bitmap," the image file format discussed in Chapter 2. *16, 31*

Bpp A measure of the number of bytes (8 bits) used to store the color of each pixel in an image. See *color depth*. *22*

bpp A measure of the number of bits used to store the color of each pixel in an image. See *color depth*. *16, 18, 22*

byte An 8-bit computational value with a storage range of 0 to 255 in decimal (00 to FF in hexadecimal). *16*

color depth A measurement of the number of bits used to indicate the color of a single pixel, also sometimes referred to as bit depth or bits per pixel (bpp). *17–19, 31*

fog of war In computer graphics, a fog of war is a graphical representation of the uncertainty of your opponents military operations. It may be represented by hidden or darkened areas of the game map that are revealed only when occupied by an active unit. *80, 183*

frame rate Number of screen draws per second, measured in frames per second (fps). Console players will expect 60 fps for action games. In old animation clips, 12 fps is considered the lowest acceptable. *22, 29*

GUI In games, the graphical user interface (GUI, commonly pronounced "gooey") usually refers to the on-screen buttons, text, gauges, and icons that allow the player to influence the events within the game. In a 3D game, the GUI is often rendered in 2D as the top layer of graphics, providing a clear boundary between the game world and the real world. *16, 96, 124*

HDTV High definition television is the newer television standard. Resolution for HTDV is measured in number of lines, for example 720p (1,280 × 720) and 1080p (1,920 × 1,080). *25, 26*

isometric projection A method of rendering three dimensions onto a two-dimensional surface such that all parallel lines along an axis have equal dimensions with the result that no foreshortening occurs. *89*

linear interpolation Interpolation is a method for finding a point on a curve, given a certain distance along that curve. The term *linear* indicates that the curve is a simple line, and as a result the curve can be evaluated from just its starting and ending points. For example, to find the point 50% along the x-axis between points $(0, 4)$ and $(10, 8)$, the resulting point $(5, 6)$ can be discovered by using the slope of the line. Sometimes called LERP for short, linear interpolation can be used to transition between Cartesian points on a grid but also between any two values, such as colors or scales, that change linearly over time, space, or other values. *140*

localization The process of ensuring a game is appropriate for a particular country or region including but not limited to language translation. *126*

pixel delta A measurement of the difference between the pixels rendered from frame to frame. For a moving sprite, this may simply be the distance between the leading edge when compared to the previous frame. For an animated sequence, it is a measure of the greatest amount of rendered movement from cel to cel (e.g., in a run cycle, it may be the relative movement of a foot from one frame to the next, measured in pixels). *62*

pixel density A measurement of the number of pixels in a physical space, commonly across a span of 1 inch: pixels per inch (ppi). In printed media, the term dots per inch (dpi) is more commonly used. *25*

raster An image comprised of individual colored pixels as opposed to points, lines, and shapes. Most computer images with which we work on a daily basis (including photographs) are raster graphics. *23, 38*

rasterization The process of converting a vector-based graphic into a bitmapped image. *38*

RGB A combination of red, green, and blue values used to define a specific color. *18*

RGBA A combination of red, green, blue, and alpha values used to define a specific color. *21*

SDTV Standard definition television (SDTV) is an older television standard, supporting either a 4:3 or 16:9 aspect ratio at resolutions equivalent to 640 × 480. *25, 26*

spline A mathematical function describing the curve of a line between two or more points.. *195*

sprite A single two-dimensional image that may be drawn as part of a larger scene. Often a single sprite is defined by the rectangular location of the image on a larger source file (sprite sheet). *17, 37*

sprite sheet A source file that includes one or more individual sprites. Sprites are grouped onto a single sprite sheet either because they are related or for efficiency during rendering. See also *atlas*. *39*

texel A texture is a 2D grid of pixels. An individual pixel on a texture may be referred to as a texel. *24*

Index